· THE ·
HOUSEPLANT
DOCTOR

· THE ·
HOUSEPLANT
DOCTOR

Andrew Bicknell and George Seddon

CHANCELLOR
PRESS

First published in Great Britain 1986
as The Houseplant Troubleshooter

This edition published in 1994
by Chancellor Press, an imprint of
Reed Consumer Books Limited, Michelin House,
81 Fulham Road, London SW3 6RB
and Auckland, Melbourne, Singapore and Toronto

ISBN 1 85152 548 3

A CIP catalogue record for this book is
available from the British Library

Printed in Italy

◇ **CONTENTS** ◇

*Unless you read this introduction you will not get full value from **The Houseplant Doctor**. The book contains an unusually large amount of information about plants presented in an unusually compact way. Several essential basic procedures and concepts, such as potting, propagation and humidity, are mentioned again and again but cannot be explained in detail each time. The following pages contain all the information you need to understand and carry out those procedures.*

PATIENT: Doctor, I have a pain in my back.
DOCTOR: Does it hurt when you're sitting or lying down?
PATIENT: No.
DOCTOR: Is the pain always in the same place?
PATIENT: Yes.
DOCTOR: Do you feel it most when you bend?
PATIENT: Yes.

And so it goes – question, answer, question, answer, the doctor probing for information about the patient's symptoms and, in most cases, reaching his conclusion by saying to himself, If it's not that, then perhaps it's this; and so on, reaching his conclusion by process of elimination.

When things go wrong with your houseplants, it is you that has to conduct this question-and-answer process. It is the best way – often the only way – to get to the root of the problem and thus to apply the

best treatment. Put like that, diagnosis sounds obvious – even easy; but of course it isn't. If a houseplant is new to you, you may not know where to start. Even if it is familiar, it is probably ailing because you are doing wrong with it. **The Houseplant Doctor** is intended to be the fastest, most convenient means of overcoming those difficulties; of turning you into a competent houseplant doctor.

You need to be honest with yourself about the way you look after your houseplants. Houseplant owners are often loathe to admit that they give anything less than the best possible care and attention to their plants. But it is true that most problems arise simply because plants have not been given the right care. Among the commonest errors are too high or too low a temperature; too much or too little water; too much or too little light; lack of humidity and irregular feeding.

Pests and diseases may also cause problems, but here again the plant owner is often to blame. Insect pests are usually introduced into the home with newly-bought plants. A useful preventive measure is to isolate these plants in a separate room for about two weeks, checking regularly for any signs of pests, before putting them back among your other plants. This routine can save you endless trouble later. Most diseases are caused in the first place by bad plant management, usually overwatering and excessive humidity, coupled with poor ventilation.

The Houseplant Doctor opens with an illustrated index/contents section. Each plant is identified by its scientifc name. This is the one to use to avoid any confusion, for that name applies to that plant and no other. If the plant has a common name, this is also given. The plant's type – whether foliage, flowering, cactus, succulent, bromeliad, orchid, fern or palm – is also given, together with an indication of the maximum size it will reach.

> The illustrated contents section

In the main section of the book, starting on **page 33**, each plant has a whole page devoted to it. There is a drawing for identification and a short description of the plant's country of origin, natural habitat and accompanying climate, all of which are valuable clues to the kind of conditions it will need in your

> The main section

home. Many houseplants originate from tropical rain forests, whose climate would both difficult and uncomfortable to imitate in the home; nonetheless, you will have to go some way toward doing just that, providing warmth and a degree of humidity, in order to keep these plants in good condition. Every plant page also gives a description of the plant's foliage and flowers, where appropriate, plus the usual time of flowering.

IDEAL CONDITIONS

The 'Ideal Conditions' summary sets out the basic needs of each plant. Provide them, and your plant should have the best chance of staying in good health:

Temperature

Suitable temperatures for summer and winter are given for each plant. Summer temperatures should be maintained for a period of several weeks either side of the season, which covers the months from mid-spring to mid-autumn. For the remainder of the year, most plants benefit from a winter rest at lower temperatures. During this period, growth will either be very slow or come to a virtual standstill. This does no harm; in fact it is positively beneficial. If plants are forced to continue growing in high temperatures but with poor and short-lived winter daylight, growth will be weak and straggly.

Far better to given them a rest, conserving their energies to put out new healthy growth in spring. Some flowering plants, cacti and orchids in particular, will flower poorly or not at all if they are not given a winter rest.

Humidity

Some plants require humidity to prevent leaf tips from turning brown. This is usually achieved by standing the pot on a tray of wet pebbles which is kept constantly topped up with water. As the water evaporates, vapour rises to the leaves above. However, the base of the pot must always be above the level of the water, otherwise the compost in the pot will become sodden and waterlogged.

An alternative method is to plunge the pot to just below the rim in a larger container filled with peat, which is kept constantly moist. The gap between the

USING THIS BOOK

There are two simple long-term methods of creating humidity around a plant. The pot can be placed on a tray of pebbles which are always kept standing in water. The base of the pot must be above the level of the water. Or the pot can be plunged in a larger container full of moist peat.

pot and the outer container must be at least 3in/7.5cm for this method to be effective. The same applies to the tray method: there is no point in using a tray which is only slightly larger than the base of the pot. Regular mist spraying of the folige also helps, but its effect is not so long lasting.

The most effective way of increasing humidity in a room is by using an electric humidifier. This will benefit all the plants, as well as the human occupants.

Most plants need bright light at all times for healthy growth, but what seems bright to us may be nowhere near bright enough for them. The brightest part of a room is the area immediately in front of a window; 6ft/2m away from the window, the light diminishes appreciably, especially if the sun is obscured by

Light

cloud. Areas of deep shade also occur either side of a window. Light-coloured walls help by reflecting bright light inward. A limited number of plants, including cacti and some flowering species, enjoy full sunlight, and some merely need shade from scorching sun.

The vast majority, however, should never be exposed to direct sunlight. A few plants, such as ferns, will be happy in shady parts of a room.

Plants with variegated leaves need plenty of light to maintain their contrasting colouring. If they do not receive it, they turn pale or revert to plain green.

Water

The advice given under this heading is not to be followed slavishly. The suggested number of times to water in summer is based on what may be necessary in periods of warm to hot weather. That frequency of watering should be maintained for a period of a few weeks either side of the three-month summer season (covering the months from late spring to early autumn). The cooler it is during this period, the less frequently plants will need to be watered. For the remainder of the year, when growth slows down and plants are resting, they use up even less water. Then, watering once a week is usually enough; for certain plants, such as cacti, the interval can be longer.

Before pouring water on to the compost, check that it really does need watering. For those plants which have to be moist all the time, looking at the surface of the compost should indicate its state, but feeling it is more reliable. It should not be dry, nor should it be sodden; just moist. If when you press the surface gently moisture appears, the compost is too wet.

For those plants where the advice is to allow the top surface of the compost to dry out between waterings, just looking at the compost surface is certainly not good enough. Stick a finger at least 1-2in/2.5-5cm into the compost and if it feels dry at that level, water is required.

The compost must be thoroughly watered every time, and that means continuing until water appears from the drainage hole in the bottom of the pot. Only then can you know that all the compost has been watered. Allow water to drain away before returning the pot to its saucer or container. Never leave pots standing in water – unless the plant happens to be *Cyperus alternifolius* or *Dionaea muscipula*.

To water plants from below place the pot in about 2in/5cm of water. Remove from the water after half an hour.

Plants may be watered from below as well as from above, and this is in fact advisable for those plants, such as saintpaulias, which have leaves that are easily marked by water.

Place the pot in about 2in/5cm of water and leave it for around half an hour until moisture appears on the surface of the compost. Remove the pot from the water and allow any excess to drain away before returning it to its saucer.

Always use tepid water; it is less of a shock to the plant's roots than cold water.

Feed

All plants should be fed regularly in the active growth period. Fresh compost contains nutrients which the plant will use up over a period of about three months; after that it will depend on you for its nourishment. Feeding should stop in autumn, when plants will be approaching their winter rest period. If you go on feeding them, encouraging them to grow in the poor light of winter, growth will become weak and straggly.

Liquid or powder fertilizers which are diluted in water are probably the easiest to use.

Always apply according to the manufacturers' instructions, never giving more than the recommended dose. Overfeeding can be fatal.

Pot-on

Potting-on simply means transferring a plant to a new pot one size larger once its roots have grown to fill the old pot. Fresh compost is used. Some plants grow so quickly that this has to be done annually. Pot sizes

To pot-on, fill the bottom of the new pot with compost to keep the plant at the level it was before. Place the old pot on the new compost and fill in the gap. Remove the pot. The root ball will fill the mould.

generally increase by 1in/2.5cm, and as a rule, plants should be potted-on to the next size up.

The easiest way to pot-on is to fill the bottom of the new pot with fresh compost to sufficient depth to keep the plant at the same level as it was before. Remove the plant from its present pot and place the empty pot on the layer of compost in the new pot. Pack the gap with compost to within about ½in/1.25cm of the rim. Remove the old pot and you are left with a mould that the root ball will almost fill. Pack with fresh compost.

If plants are not potted-on every year, they should certainly be repotted annually to renew the compost. Remove the plant from the pot and gently break away some of the old compost from the roots. Do not disturb the roots too much. Return the plant to a pot of the same size and firm down the roots in the fresh compost.

Propagation

Stem cuttings should be about 4in/10cm long. Trim off the bottom pair of leaves, dip in rooting powder and plant in compost.

Under this heading, advice is given on the method of propagation and the time of the year at which to do it; this is usually spring.

The simplest form of propagation is division, where a plant is divided into two pieces. Do not divide a plant into many puny pieces; it will be months before they look presentable again. To divide, remove the plant from the pot and gently prise the roots apart. Repot each section in fresh compost.

Some plants grow from rhizomes and tubers, fleshy stems growing either underneath or on the surface of the compost, which can be divided. Remove the rhizome or tuber from the pot and cut it into pieces; each must have several buds. Fill a tray with compost, followed by a layer of sharp (coarse) sand and place the pieces on top. Cover the tray with a sheet of plastic and keep it in the warmth. When growth appears from the buds, plant in compost.

Offsets grow from the base of some plants. They can be cut away from the main plant and must have enough roots to support them.

Plants on runners, such as chlorophytums, should be pinned down into compost and severed from the main plant when roots have developed.

The plantlets of tolmiea, which grow at the junction of leaf and stalk, are rooted by removing a complete

Top left: **An offset can be removed when about 9in/22.5cm long. It must have enough roots to support it or it will not grow. Illustrated is** *Clivia miniata.*

Middle: **Runners can be pinned down into a pot of compost. When they have rooted and are growing well sever them from the parent plant. Illustrated is** *Chlorophytum comosum.*

Bottom: **Stems of cacti are easy to propagate. Hold the stem with thick layers of paper and cut it off with a sharp knife. Leave to dry out for a day or two and plant in compost. Illustrated is** *Opuntia microdasys.*

Top right: **Rhizomes can be divided to make new plants. Each piece must have several buds. Place the pieces on a tray filled with a layer of compost topped with a layer of sharp sand.**

Leaves of *Begonia rex* can be propagated by pinning down a whole leaf in sand. Make a few shallow cuts into the veins on the underside of the leaf. Pin it down with loops of wire. Small plants will appear from the cuts.

Cuttings will root more easily if they are enclosed in a plastic bag punched with holes. Support the bag with four canes and place an elastic band round the pot rim to secure the open end. The cutting must not touch the plastic.

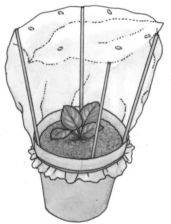

leaf and stalk. Cut the stalk down to 2in/5cm and stick it into compost so that the leaf lies on the compost surface. Roots will soon develop on the small plantlet.

Cacti and succulent offsets are left to dry out for a few days after cutting away and then planted in compost.

Stem cuttings from soft-stemmed plants should be about 4in/10cm long, with at least three pairs of leaves. Make the cut just below the point where a leaf joins the stem. Trim off the bottom pair of leaves, dip the stem into hormone rooting powder and plant in compost. Cover the cutting with a plastic bag, with holes punched in it and supported by four canes, and secure the open end with an elastic band around the pot rim. The cutting should not touch the plastic. Some cuttings require constant high temperatures before they will strike – a heated propagator will provide the necessary bottom heat.

Cuttings from plants with woody stems should be about the same size, but taken with a heel – a small piece of the main stem bark. Select a suitable side shoot and tug it downward sharply. Trim the heel, dip the cutting in rooting powder and plant it in compost. Cover it with a plastic bag.

Dry out cacti and succulent stem cuttings for a few days before planting in compost. They require a temperature of 70°F/21°C, but should not be covered.

Saintpaulia ionantha, African violet, can be propagated from leaf cuttings. Break off a leaf and stalk, trim the stalk to 1in/2.5cm, dip in rooting powder and plant in compost at a 45° angle. Cover the pot with a plastic bag. Propagate the leaves of *Begonia rex* in the same way, or pin down a whole leaf in sand. Select a healthy leaf, turn it over and, on the underside, make a few shallow cuts into the veins. Pin the leaf down on sand with a few loops of wire, the cut surface touching the sand. Cover with a plastic bag and keep in a temperature of 70°F/21°C. Small plants will emerge from the cut veins.

Many plants can be raised from seed, but heat is often needed to make the seed germinate and here a heated propagator is the answer. If considerable heat is required, this fact is mentioned in the text. To maintain humidity, all other seeds should be covered with plastic that is punched with holes and kept as warm as possible. Fill the seed tray with 2in/5cm of loam- or peat-based seed compost. Large seed should be covered with a thin layer of compost and fine seed with sand.

Wet the compost by immersing the tray in water up to its rim until moisture appears on the surface. Place in a propagator or cover with plastic. Do not let the compost dry out and do not expose to direct sun. When the first true leaves appear, transplant the seedlings into pots of compost.

Ferns are difficult to propagate from spores but it is worth a try. Detach a frond which has brown spore cases on the underside. Keep in a bag in the dark

until the spore cases dry out, releasing the spores. Scatter the spores on a tray of peat moss and cover with a plastic bag. Keep in the warmth, with good light, and after a few weeks there will be a green film covering the peat moss, the first stage of growth. Maintain humidity and warmth and you may be rewarded with the first recognizable fronds.

PROBLEM

Problem diagnosis

The greater part of each page is given over to diagnosing problems. For every plant, the diagnosis begins with the problem or symptom(s) most likely to occur with that plant. There are, in fact, a limited number of obvious symptoms, probably the most common being leaf tips turning brown, brown marks on the leaves or leaves shrivelling and falling.

But though the symptoms may be the same, the causes can be various. They range from lack of humidity, overwatering, underwatering, temperatures too high or low, depending on the particular plant and the quality of care it has had.

If you answer 'yes' to the first question, the problem has been solved and action to be taken to restore the plant to health – if possible – is then given.

If you answer 'no', you go on until you have tracked down the cause. When working your way through these sequences, never lose sight of the original problem posed; keep going back to the top of the page.

Some plants may confront you with more than one problem, in which case work through the problems listed until you find yours – and the cure.

At the foot of some pages is a box labelled 'Other species'. This mentions further notable plants of the genus: they may well be varieties of the main plant with slightly differing foliage or flower colour. If you have a plant of a genus mentioned in the book but the particular species or variety is not included, you may assume that the care details, problems and requirements for cure will be the same.

CALENDAR		
Northern hemisphere		**Southern hemisphere**
Actual month	Season given in text	Actual month
January	Winter	June
February	Late winter	July
March	Early spring	August
April	Spring	September
May	Late spring	October
June	Early summer	November
July	Summer	December
August	Late summer	January
September	Early autumn	February
October	Autumn	March
November	Late autumn	April
December	Early winter	May

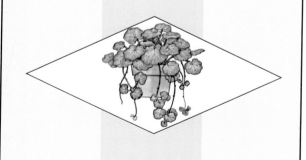

CONTENTS

CONTENTS

C

◆ **CONTENTS** ◆

CONTENTS

Calathea makoyana,
Peacock plant.
Foliage. To 2ft/60cm.
Page 60

Callisia elegans,
Striped inch plant.
Foliage trailer.
To 2ft/60cm.
Page 61

Campanula isophylla
'Mayi', Bell flower.
Flowering perennial.
To 12in/30cm.
Page 62

Capsicum annuum,
Chili pepper. Fruiting.
To 9in/22.5cm.
Page 63

Cattleya bowringiana,
Cluster cattleya.
Orchid. To 12in/30cm.
Page 64

Cephalocereus senilis,
Old man cactus.
To 12in/30cm.
Page 65

Chamaedorea elegans,
Parlour palm; Good
luck palm. To 4ft/1.2m.
Page 66

Chamaerops humilis,
European fan palm.
To 5ft/1.5m.
Page 67

*Chlorophytum
comosum* 'Vittatum',
Spider plant.
Foliage trailer.
To 2ft/60cm.
Page 68

C

◆ **CONTENTS** ◆

***Chrysalidocarpus
lutescens,*** Areca palm.
Fronds to 4ft/1.2m.
Spread to 6ft/1.8m.
Page 69

Cissus antarctica,
Kangaroo vine. Foliage
trailer. To 10ft/3m.
Page 70

Citrus mitis,
Calamondin orange.
Fruiting. To 3ft/90cm.
Page 71

Clivia miniata,
Kaffir lily. Flowering.
Leaves to 2ft/60cm.
Spread 3ft/90cm.
Page 72

***Codiaeum variegatum
pictum,*** Croton.
Foliage. To 3ft/90cm.
Page 73

Coleus blumei,
Flame nettle. Foliage.
To 18in/45cm.
Page 74

***Columnea
microphylla,*** Goldfish
vine. Flowering trailer.
To 3ft/90cm.
Page 75

Cordyline terminalis
'Rededge', Hawaiian ti
plant. Foliage. Grows
to 2ft/60cm.
Page 76

Crassula aborescens,
Silver dollar plant.
Succulent. Grows
to 3ft/90cm.
Page 77

CONTENTS

CONTENTS

CONTENTS

CONTENTS

CONTENTS

CONTENTS

CONTENTS

CONTENTS

CONTENTS

TROUBLESHOOTING SECTION

All 128 plants are arranged
alphabetically, one to a page

◆ **PROBLEM** ◆

Are the leaves curling and turning brown at the tips?

────── IF YES ──────

CAUSE Lack of humidity.
ACTION Create a humid atmosphere around the plant: see page 8. Spray plants daily, except when they are in flower.

────── IF NO ──────

When you push a finger into the compost does it feel dry below the surface?

────── IF YES ──────

CAUSE The plant has been kept too dry, causing the leaves to curl and wilt.
ACTION Water the compost thoroughly. Allow any excess to drain away through the hole in the bottom of the pot before putting the pot back on its saucer. Thereafter water as in **IDEAL CONDITIONS**. The compost should always be moist.

────── IF NO ──────

As well as leaves curling, are their surfaces covered with yellow spots and fine white webs?

────── IF YES ──────

CAUSE Red spider mites have been attracted by the dryness of the air. These creatures, the size of a pin-head, suck sap from the leaves, producing the yellow spots; in severe infestations, fine white webs are visible on the leaves.
ACTION Spray the plant with liquid derris. All badly affected parts should be removed. You may have to repeat the treatment every few days until all signs of the pests have disappeared. Then, to keep them at bay, maintain a constant humid atmosphere.

────── **PROBLEM** ──────

Has the plant refused to flower in spring and summer?

────── IF YES ──────

CAUSE It has not had sufficient light.
ACTION Place the plant in a sunny window, but shade it from the hottest sun. Acalyphas with variegated leaves will also lose their colour if they do not get enough light.

Acalypha hispida
Acalyphas are native to the steamy forests of New Guinea, in the western Pacific. Summer is hot and humid, up to 80°F/27°C by day, a little cooler at night, with similar temperatures in winter. Rain falls all year round. Leaves are bright green and hairy; red tassel-like flowers appear from late spring to early autumn.

IDEAL CONDITIONS

Temperature 65-70°F/18-21°C all year; but a winter rest down to 60°F/16°C does the plant no harm.
Light Bright, with direct sun for good flowering. Shade from the fiercest sun.
Water Two or three times a week in summer to keep the compost moist, once a week in winter. Needs a humid atmosphere.
Feed Every two weeks, from spring to early autumn.
Pot-on Every spring in peat-based compost.
Propagation Take stem-tip cuttings; these require a temperature of 75°F/24°C to root.

**A
C
H
I
M
E
N
E
S**

Achimenes longiflora
Achimenes comes from
Central America, in
particular Mexico and
Honduras, where
summer temperatures
reach 80°F/27°C, falling
a few degrees at night.
Blue, purple, pink or
white flowers,
depending on the
cultivar, appear from
early spring to early
autumn. The plant has a
dormant period after
flowering.

IDEAL CONDITIONS

Temperature
65°F/18°C to bring
the rhizome into
growth; 55-65°F/13-
18°C once growth is
established. In winter,
store the rhizomes at
50°F/10°C.
Light Bright, but
away from direct sun.
Water Two or three
times a week to keep
the compost
thoroughly moist.
Stored rhizomes
should be kept
completely dry.
Feed Every two
weeks in spring and
summer.
Pot-on Every spring
in peat-based
compost.
Propagation Either
divide the rhizome
when potting-on or
take stem cuttings in
early summer.

PROBLEM

Has the plant refused to flower, or have the
flower buds turned brown and failed to open?

IF YES

CAUSE The plant has not been getting enough water.
ACTION After the rhizomes have been potted-on in
spring, the compost should be kept just moist. Once
new growth has emerged, water more frequently so
that the compost is thoroughly moist all the time. If the
compost becomes too dry, the rhizomes may revert to
dormancy. After flowering, foliage and stems die
down in preparation for dormancy; when all the
foliage is dead, cut it off at compost level. Either store
the rhizomes, completely dry, in the compost until the
following spring or remove them from the compost
and store dry in sand. The ideal storage temperature
is 50°F/10°C. Do not expose rhizomes to frost.

IF NO

Has the plant been in direct sunlight in a hot room?

IF YES

CAUSE Too much heat has caused the flower buds to
turn brown.
ACTION This plant will tolerate a wide temperature
range of up to 80°F/27°C, but beyond that the flower
buds will be affected.

PROBLEM

Has the plant begun to look straggly, with long trailing
stems?

IF YES

CAUSE This is the natural habit of the plant, but it can be
trained to grow bushy.
ACTION Any overlong stems can be cut to 6in/15cm
and then pinched out once there is good growth.

OTHER SPECIES
Achimenes longiflora 'Alba' has white flowers
with purple centres.
Achimenes grandiflora has large hairy leaves
and reddish-purple flowers.
Achimenes erecta has small leaves and bright
red flowers.

PROBLEM

Have the leaves turned brown, shrivelled and fallen from the fronds? Does the compost feel dry?

IF YES

CAUSE The compost has not been kept thoroughly moist.

ACTION Water the compost, allowing excess water to drain away through the hole in the bottom of the pot. Cut down all the fronds to near compost level and spray the stubble every day. Eventually new fronds will appear. Then follow the instructions about watering in **IDEAL CONDITIONS**.

IF NO

Has the plant been in a dry atmosphere?

IF YES

CAUSE Lack of humidity.

ACTION Either stand the pot on a tray of wet pebbles or surround it with peat, kept constantly moist. A daily overhead mist spray will also help.

IF NO

Has the plant been in a sunny window?

IF YES

CAUSE Direct sunlight will make the leaves turn pale and wither.

ACTION Cut away badly damaged fronds at compost level and move the plant out of direct sun, but place it in a good light.

PROBLEM

Does the plant look pale and weak in spring/summer?

IF YES

CAUSE Lack of nutrients.

ACTION Start feeding the plant regularly – every three to four weeks throughout spring and summer. Foliage will soon turn a darker green, and the plant will begin to recover its health.

OTHER SPECIES

Adiantum cuneatum (syn *raddianum*), from Brazil, has larger fronds, about 18in/45cm long, with coarser leaflets.

Adiantum capillus-veneris

Adiantums are found in temperate areas, such as Britain and the USA, and in cooler parts of tropical areas. Summer temperatures are 55-60°F/13-16°C, or higher; winter temperatures are around 45-50°F/7-10°C. There is rainfall throughout the year. The foliage is delicately lacy, on black wiry stems.

IDEAL CONDITIONS

Temperature In spring and summer 60-65°F/16-18°C; 55°F/13°C in the winter rest period. The plant will suffer below 50°F/10°C.

Light Bright, but away from direct sun.

Water Twice a week in summer, so the compost is always moist, once in winter. Needs humidity.

Feed Once every three to four weeks in spring and summer.

Pot-on In spring in a mixture of peat, loam and sand, or peat-based compost.

Propagation Divide in spring. Raise from the spores on undersides of leaves. Difficult, and needs bottom heat of 70°F/21°C.

Aechmea fasciata
Aechmeas are found in forest areas of Brazil. They are epiphytic plants, anchored by their roots to branches of trees or to rocks. They will thrive in a pot, but they can also be grown fastened to a suitable branch if the roots are bound in sphagnum moss. Leaves grey-green, banded silver. Spike of pink bracts.

IDEAL CONDITIONS

Temperature
70°F/21°C all year, but try to give the plant a rest in winter at 55-60°F/13-16°C.
Light Bright with some direct sun unless it is scorching.
Water Twice a week and keep the central urn of the plant full of water. Change the water in the urn every two to three weeks so that it stays fresh. In winter months, water once a month and keep the urn dry. Spray daily in warm weather.
Feed Once a month, spring and summer.
Pot-on No. Main plant dies after flowering, leaving offsets.
Propagation Detach and pot-up offsets when well grown.

PROBLEM

Have the leaves and flower stem started to wither? Check the compost. Does it feel wet?

IF YES

CAUSE The compost has been watered too frequently.
ACTION Empty water from the centre of the urn and let the compost dry out. If the rot has gone too far, resign yourself to losing the plant. Rotting can be avoided by letting the compost dry out between waterings, and in winter the central urn must not be filled with water. Keep the plant in a well-ventilated position.

IF NO

Has the plant finished flowering and are the bright pink bracts starting to fade?

IF YES

CAUSE Withering after flowering is natural.
ACTION The plant gradually dies, but small offsets appear at the base. When well established, they can be cut away, but make sure they have some root structure, small though it may be. Plant offsets in a mixture of loam, peat and leaf-mould. Do not use composts which contain lime. You may have to wait two or three years before an offset produces flowers.

IF NO

Has the plant been in a hot room with direct sun?

IF YES

CAUSE The plant has become dehydrated because of excessive heat.
ACTION Water the compost liberally, allowing excess water to drain through the drainage hole in the pot. Fill the central urn with fresh water, preferably rainwater, since the lime in hard water marks the leaves. Spray the plant, also using rain water. Move it out of the line of direct sun. Always shade an aechmea from scorching sun.

OTHER SPECIES
Aechmea fulgens has olive-green leaves with deep purple undersides; purple flowers, red berries.
Aechmea chantinii has grey-green leaves with white bands; yellow flowers, orange-red bracts.

Agave americana
Agaves are succulents, native to dry, semi-desert areas of Mexico, where the rainfall is extremely erratic. The fleshy leaves, grey-green and strap-shaped, store water, so the plants are able to survive for many weeks between the downpours. Temperatures can be very high by day, dropping to give ground frost at night.

PROBLEM

Are the leaves covered with brown and yellow soft spots? Do the leaves at the base of the rosette feel soft and mushy when gently pressed?

IF YES

CAUSE The plant has been watered too much and is suffering from stem rot disease.
ACTION If all the leaves are affected at the base of the rosette, throw the plant away. For minor attacks, remove the rotten leaves cleanly from the rosette. If any rot is left behind, further rot is likely to set in. Dust the compost with fungicide powder or soak it with benomyl. Let the compost dry out for several days before watering again and then follow watering instructions in **IDEAL CONDITIONS**.

IF NO

Has the plant been kept in a poorly ventilated room?

IF YES

CAUSE Poor ventilation, along with excessive humidity, causes leaf spot disease.
ACTION Badly infected leaves should be removed, and the plant sprayed with benomyl or thiophanate-methyl. Either ventilate the room better or move the plant to a more airy place.

PROBLEM

Are there dry brown spots on the leaves and does the plant have a generally shrivelled appearance? When you push a finger into the compost does it feel dry just under the surface?

IF YES

CAUSE The plant is not getting enough water. Agaves store water in their fleshy leaves, but when they have used up this reserve the leaves begin to shrivel.
ACTION The leaves will be permanently scarred, but unless they are badly affected they should not be removed. Water the compost thoroughly. Allow excess water to drain away before returning the pot to its saucer. In the future, follow watering instructions in **IDEAL CONDITIONS**.

OTHER SPECIES

Agave americana 'Marginata' has yellow leaf margins.

IDEAL CONDITIONS

Temperature
65-70°F/18-21°C, but rest plants in winter months at around 50-55°F/10-13°C.
Light Bright, but shade from direct sun.
Water Once or twice a week. Allow the surface of compost to dry out between waterings. When the plant is resting, water only once or twice a month.
Feed Once a month from spring to early autumn.
Pot-on Every other year in spring in loam-based compost, with added sand for free drainage.
Propagation Detach offsets at the base of the plant, or sow seed in spring.

Aglaonema crispum
'Silver Queen'
Aglaonemas are natives of Southeast Asia, especially the warm damp forests of the Philippines and Malaysia. Temperatures to 80°F/27°C and rain all the year round. The plant tolerates partial shade but must have humidity and warmth. The oval leaves are dark green and leathery, marked with silver.

IDEAL CONDITIONS

Temperature 65-75°F/18-24°C all year. It will not thrive below 60°F/16°C.
Light Does not mind a slightly shaded spot. Never expose to direct sunlight.
Water Twice a week in spring and summer. Once a week at other times.
Feed Every two weeks in spring and summer.
Pot-on Every other year in spring in peat-based compost. Change compost for fresh in the year between.
Propagation Divide when potting-on or take stem cuttings in summer.

PROBLEM

Have the leaves become dry and papery, with browning of the edges?

IF YES

CAUSE The atmosphere is too dry.
ACTION Aglaonemas require high humidity throughout the year. Stand the pot on a tray of wet pebbles or surround it with moist peat. Spray the plant daily.

IF NO

Has the plant been exposed to the sun?

IF YES

CAUSE Hot direct sun scorches the leaves.
ACTION Move the plant to a shady part of the room or protect it from fierce sun behind a translucent blind.

PROBLEM

Have the leaves turned yellow?

IF YES

CAUSE The plant has been left in an unheated room in winter or has been in too low a temperature over a period of time. A combination of low temperatures and wet compost causes leaves to yellow.
ACTION Bring the plant into a room with temperatures of 65-75°F/18-24°C. Allow the compost to dry out and water as in **IDEAL CONDITIONS**.

PROBLEM

Are there white woolly patches on the undersides of leaves and on the stems?

IF YES

CAUSE These woolly patches are the protective homes of mealy bugs that suck sap from the leaves, turning them yellow and causing wilt.
ACTION Spray plants with liquid derris and remove any badly infected leaves.

OTHER SPECIES
Aglaonema commutatum 'Treubii', grey-green leaves marked with yellow.
Anglaonema commutatum pseudobracteatum, elongated oval green leaves marked grey-green and white to yellow.

◇ **PROBLEM** ◇

Do the leaves at the base of the rosette feel soft and mushy if gently pressed?

IF YES

CAUSE The plant has been watered directly on the rosette of leaves, inducing stem and crown rot disease.

ACTION If only a few leaves have been affected, the plant may be saved, but if the whole crown – the base of the rosette – is rotting the plant should be discarded. For mild attacks, remove the rotting leaves cleanly; any pieces left behind will encourage further rot to set in. Dust the compost with fungicide powder or soak it with benomyl. Allow the compost to dry out for a few days before watering again. This plant is best watered from below. Put about 2in/5cm of water in a basin and stand the pot in it for half an hour – until moisture is seen on the surface of the compost. Allow excess water to drain out before returning the pot to its saucer.

PROBLEM

Do the leaves look soft and bloated? If you push a finger into the compost does it feel wet just below the surface?

IF YES

CAUSE The plant has been overwatered.

ACTION Allow the compost to dry out almost completely before watering again, but if the leaves still feel bloated, do not water. The plant has too much water in reserve which it must first use up.

PROBLEM

Are the leaves beginning to shrivel? When you push a finger into the compost does it feel dry just below the surface?

IF YES

CAUSE The plant is not getting enough water. All the water reserve in the leaves has been used up, and they are becoming dehydrated.

ACTION Water the plant thoroughly and subsequently follow the watering routine in **IDEAL CONDITIONS**. There will then be no need for the plant to call upon its emergency reserves of water, with possible damage to the leaves.

Aloe variegata
The aloe is a succulent from South Africa. It thrives in bush areas, with long hot summers, 70°F/21°C, and mild winters, 55°F/13°C. Most rain falls in winter, and the leaves store water against dry summers. The leaves are triangular, green with white bands. Tubular pink flowers in spring and summer.

IDEAL CONDITIONS

Temperature 65-70°F/18-21°C throughout the year, but plants are more likely to flower if given a winter rest at 45-50°F/8-10°C.
Light Bright, but no direct sun. Other aloe species like direct sun.
Water Twice a week to keep the compost evenly moist but not sodden. Once a month in winter if in low temperature; more frequently if in normal room temperature.
Feed Once a month, spring and summer.
Pot-on Every two or three years in loam-based compost.
Propagation Remove offsets at the base of the plant.

ANANAS

Ananas comosus variegatus
Ananas, the pineapple, is a terrestrial bromeliad which originated in Brazil. Summers are hot and humid, with heavy thundery rain, but there is some rain all year round. The tooth-edged leaves are grey-green with white to yellow margins. Plants are customarily on sale after the fruit has appeared, following a spike of purple flowers.

IDEAL CONDITIONS

Temperature All year at 65-75°F/ 18-24°C, since the plant does not seem to need a winter rest; it will tolerate winter temperatures down to 60°F/16°C.
Light As much direct sunlight as possible all year for good leaf colour.
Water Once or twice a week in summer, and in winter also if the room is warm. Compost should be evenly moist always.
Feed Every two to three weeks in spring and summer.
Pot-on In spring in lime-free loam compost with added leaf-mould.
Propagation Detach the offsets from the base of the plant.

PROBLEM

Are the leaf tips turning brown? Do they feel dry and brittle? Are the leaves shrivelling and curling?

IF YES

CAUSE The air is too dry.
ACTION Spray the plant daily, especially during hot weather. Stand the pot in a container of moist peat.

IF NO

Has the plant been near a door which is left open frequently, causing cold draughts?

IF YES

CAUSE A combination of draughts and low temperatures will make the lower leaves dry out and shrivel.
ACTION Move the plant away from possible draughts to a place with a temperature of 65-75°F/18-24°C. Leaves that are completely shrivelled should be removed cleanly from the base of the plant. If a leaf has only a brown tip, cut this away but do not cut into the healthy green part of the leaf; to do so would hasten the death of the whole leaf.

PROBLEM

Do the leaves at the base of the plant feel soft and mushy?

IF YES

CAUSE The compost has become waterlogged.
ACTION Let the compost dry out thoroughly. Remove any rotten stems and dust the compost with a fungicide. Badly infected plants should be thrown away. Pineapples need a very free-draining compost.

PROBLEM

After the miniature pineapple fruit has died, is the rest of the plant starting to shrivel and die?

IF YES

CAUSE This is natural. Once the plant has produced flowers and fruit it dies down, but as it dies, it throws out offsets, small replicas of itself, from the base.
ACTION Allow the offsets to become well established, at least 6in/15cm high. Then cut them away cleanly with a knife. Plant in lime-free loam-based compost to which well-rotted leaf-mould has been added to make it more porous.

PROBLEM

Have the leaf tips turned brown, and are the leaves curling and becoming papery? Has the plant refused to flower?

=== IF YES ===

CAUSE The air is too dry.
ACTION Create a humid atmosphere around the plant either by standing the pot on a tray of wet pebbles or by surrounding it with peat which is always kept moist. Regular spraying will also help.

=== IF NO ===

Is the surface of the leaves covered with yellow spots and fine white webs?

=== IF YES ===

CAUSE The plant is being attacked by red spider mites, encouraged by a dry atmosphere. These small insects suck sap from the leaves, producing yellow spots, and they deposit white webs around the leaves and stems.
ACTION Remove any badly affected parts of the plant. Spray with liquid derris. The treatment should be repeated every few days if signs of the insects persist. To prevent further attacks, maintain a humid atmosphere as described earlier.

=== PROBLEM ===

Are the leaf edges or the whole leaf turning yellow?

=== IF YES ===

CAUSE The plant has been kept too wet and exposed to a low temperature or a sudden temperature drop.
ACTION Move the plant to a room where the temperature is 65-75°F/18-24°C. Allow the compost to become almost dry before watering again. In future, water as in **IDEAL CONDITIONS**.

=== PROBLEM ===

Are the newly produced leaves pale and not growing as large as the previous leaves?

=== IF YES ===

CAUSE The plant is not being fed regularly.
ACTION Apply a liquid feed to the compost. The plant should be fed every two weeks over the whole period from late spring to early autumn. Do not feed for the remainder of the year when the plant is resting.

Anthurium scherzerianum
The anthurium is native to the steamy rain forest areas of Central America. Temperatures are constant, around 75°F/24°C, and the rainfall high all year, so plants go on growing with no rest. The leaves are lance-shaped and leathery; orange-red flower spikes emerge from spathes of the same colour from early spring to summer.

IDEAL CONDITIONS

Temperature All year in the range 65-70°F/18-21°C. In winter they tolerate temperatures down to 60°F/16°C.
Light Bright, but not direct sunlight.
Water Twice a week in summer to ensure the compost is always moist. Once a week in winter, but more frequently if room temperatures are high. Needs a humid atmosphere.
Feed Every two weeks from late spring to early autumn.
Pot-on Every spring in a peat-based compost with some sphagnum moss added.
Propagation Divide in spring.

A P H E L A N D R A

Aphelandra squarrosa 'Louisae'
Aphelandras came from the rain forests of Brazil and thrive in warm, wet conditions. They have bright yellow bracts, tipped with orange, from which flowers of the same colour emerge in summer. Flowers usually last for around three weeks. These plants are often discarded after flowering, but, with care, may flower a second year.

IDEAL CONDITIONS

Temperature Spring to autumn 65-70°F/18-21°C. Rest the plant for the remainder of the year at around 60°F/16°C.
Light Bright, but away from direct sun.
Water Twice a week when in active growth so that the compost is always moist. Once a week in rest period, but compost must never dry out completely.
Feed Once every two weeks from late spring to early autumn.
Pot-on In spring in a peat-based compost.
Propagation From stem cuttings taken in late spring.

PROBLEM

Are the leaves drooping? First test the compost; when you push a finger in does it feel moist just below the surface?

IF YES

CAUSE The leaves droop naturally; only excessive drooping would suggest the plant is short of water.
ACTION If with the finger test you have found the compost moist, there is no need to water.

PROBLEM

Are the edges of the leaves turning brown?

IF YES

CAUSE The air is too dry.
ACTION To increase humidity around the plant, stand the pot on a tray of wet pebbles or surround it with moist peat.

PROBLEM

Are the leaves falling?

IF YES

CAUSE The compost has been allowed to dry out.
ACTION Thoroughly water the compost. Allow excess water to drain away through the drainage hole in the bottom of the pot before returning it to its saucer.

IF NO

Has the plant been standing near an open door or in an unheated room?

IF YES

CAUSE Draughts and too low temperatures make leaves fall and may kill the plant.
ACTION Move the plant to a draught-free spot in a room where the temperature is 65-70°F/18-21°C. Aphelandras will tolerate a temperature down to 60°F/16°C, but certainly no lower.

PROBLEM

After flowering, have the bracts turned green?

IF YES

CAUSE This is the natural habit of the plant.
ACTION If you want to keep the plant for another year, cut back stems by a quarter to just above a pair of leaves. New growth will emerge here next spring.

PROBLEM

Are flower buds dropping; do stems look weak and spindly?

Aporocactus flagelliformis
The aporocactus is found in desert areas of Mexico. Daytime temperature may be 90°F/30°C or more, falling dramatically at night. Rainfall is erratic, but the green fleshy stems, covered in brown spines, store water against times of drought. Deep pink tubular flowers bloom in spring and early summer.

─────── **IF YES** ───────

CAUSE The plant has been put in a poorly lit spot.
ACTION It is too late to do anything this year; resign yourself to the fact that the plant will not flower. For the future, bring the plant into a temperature of 65°F/18°C in early spring and place it in a good light with as much direct sun as possible. A period outdoors in summer benefits the plant.

─────── **PROBLEM** ───────

Are there no signs of flower buds in early spring?

─────── **IF YES** ───────

CAUSE The plant has not had a winter rest.
ACTION Make sure that next winter the plant is given winter relief as in **IDEAL CONDITIONS**.

─────── **PROBLEM** ───────

Do the stems feel soft at the base?

─────── **IF YES** ───────

CAUSE The plant has been watered too much, especially in winter, making the stems rot. When plants are resting at low temperatures, they need far less water than when they are in active growth.
ACTION Remove all totally rotten stems and cut away soft areas of less affected stems. Brush the cuts with a fungicide powder and dust the compost with it.

─────── **PROBLEM** ───────

Does the plant look pale and shrivelled?

─────── **IF YES** ───────

CAUSE The plant is not getting enough water.
ACTION Give the compost a good soaking and in future water according to instructions in **IDEAL CONDITIONS**.

─────── **IF NO** ───────

Has the plant been fed regularly?

─────── **IF NO** ───────

CAUSE The plant has been undernourished.
ACTION Start feeding the plant once a month between spring and early autumn, with high-potash fertilizer.

IDEAL CONDITIONS

Temperature Around 65°F/18°C from early spring to early autumn. Rest the plant in winter at around 50°F/10°C.
Light Bright with direct sun.
Water Twice a week in spring and summer to keep compost constantly moist. Every two weeks in winter in a cool room.
Feed Monthly, spring to early autumn.
Pot-on Each year after flowering in peat-based compost or a mixture of three parts loam to one part sand.
Propagation Take stem cuttings in summer. Let cuttings dry a few days before potting.

APOROCACTUS

Araucaria excelsa
The araucaria comes from Norfolk Island, northwest of New Zealand. In summer, temperatures are 65-75°F/18-24°C; in winter, 43-50°F/6-10°C. Rain falls throughout the year. This is a slow-growing, evergreen conifer, with tiers of bright green horizontal branches sprouting from a woody stem in groups of four or more.

IDEAL CONDITIONS

Temperature 55-65°F/13-18°C from spring to early autumn; the lower temperatures are better. In winter around 50°F/10°C; not below 40°F/4°C.
Light Bright, but away from direct sun.
Water Twice a week in spring and summer to keep compost evenly moist. Every 7 to 10 days in winter.
Feed Every two weeks, late spring to early autumn.
Pot-on Every third year in loam-based compost. Change compost each year.
Propagation Sow seeds in spring. It will be a long time before the plant reaches a fair size.

PROBLEM

Have the needles turned yellow and started to fall?

IF YES

CAUSE The plant has been kept too warm.
ACTION Find a cooler part of the room for it or a cooler room. It is difficult to regulate temperatures in spring and summer, but the plant needs one no higher than 65°F/18°C and does better if it is nearer 55°F/13°C. In warm weather, spray plants daily, using rainwater if the water is hard, since lime marks the leaves.

IF NO

Is the plant in a very shady part of the room?

IF YES

CAUSE The plant is not getting enough light.
ACTION Move the plant closer to the window. The araucaria should not be exposed to direct sunlight, but good light is needed for healthy growth.

PROBLEM

Have the lower leaves started to fall?

IF YES

CAUSE The plant has been kept too warm during its winter rest period and has had too much water.
ACTION Move the plant to a cooler room – around 50°F/10°C and not lower than 40°F/4°C. In such conditions water only when the compost feels dry. Lower leaves that have fallen will not be replaced, since new growth appears at the top of the stem.

PROBLEM

Is the plant losing its symmetrical shape as it grows?

IF YES

CAUSE The plant is not getting the same amount of light all around, and plants always grow toward the light. Outdoors they will grow upward and evenly, but indoors, where there is no light from above, they will turn toward a window. This is most likely to happen in the short daylight hours of winter.
ACTION Move the plant as close as possible to a window in winter and turn the pot regularly, a little at a time, so that all sides of the plant get an equal share of what light there is. But do not expose it to direct sun.

PROBLEM

Have the berries started to fall soon after turning red?

Ardisia crenata
Ardisia, the coral berry, is native to an area from the East Indies to Japan that is warm in summer, 65-75°F/18-24°C, cool in winter, 43-50°F/6-10°C. Rain falls throughout the year. Narrow, glossy dark green leaves; small fragrant red flowers in summer and red berries, which last for weeks in winter, given the right treatment.

IF YES

CAUSE The plant has been kept too warm.
ACTION Move the plant to a room with a temperature of about 50°F/10°C. If this is not possible, keep the plant as cool as you can and provide a humid atmosphere by standing the pot on a tray of wet pebbles or placing it in a container of moist peat. Regular spraying of the leaves will also help. There will then be less likelihood of the berries falling.

IF NO

Has the plant been near an open door or one that is frequently opened?

IF YES

CAUSE The plant is suffering from a draught.
ACTION Simply move the plant out of the draught.

IF NO

When you push a finger into the compost, does it feel dry an inch or so below the surface?

IF YES

CAUSE The plant has been kept too dry.
ACTION Water the compost thoroughly and allow excess water to drain away before returning the pot to its saucer. Thereafter, check the compost regularly and follow the watering instructions set out in **IDEAL CONDITIONS**.

PROBLEM

Has the plant grown leggy and lost its lower leaves?

IF YES

CAUSE As the plant ages, it is natural for some of the lower leaves to fall. Eventually the stem may be bare, with a few leaves at the top, which looks most unattractive.
ACTION Cut back the stem to within 3in/7.5cm of the compost. This may seem drastic, but new growth will soon appear from the cut-down stem. The operation is best carried out in the spring when the plant is starting its natural surge of growth; it should rapidly re-establish itself and put out new leaves.

IDEAL CONDITIONS

Temperature From spring to early autumn 55-65°F/13-18°C; in winter about 50°F/10°C.
Light Bright, but no direct sun.
Water Twice a week, spring to early autumn to keep compost always moist. In winter, every two weeks if the plant is in a cool room.
Feed Every two weeks from spring to early autumn.
Pot-on Every spring, in loam-based compost with some leaf-mould added.
Propagation Take heel cuttings in summer or sow seed in spring, but it will be about three years before flowers and fruit appear.

Asparagus densiflorus 'Sprengeri'
The asparagus fern is a native of Natal, S. Africa, where summers are quite warm, up to 65°F/18°C, and winters cool, down to 45°F/7°C. Rainfall is low, most of it in summer, and the winters fairly dry. The plant has developed fleshy tuberous roots that hold reserves of water, enabling it to survive drought.

IDEAL CONDITIONS

Temperature All year 55-65°F/13-18°C, but 55°F/13°C is best. In winter can survive down to 45°F/7°C.
Light Bright, but no direct sun.
Water Two or three times a week to keep the compost moist throughout. In winter, once a week; less in low temperatures. Compost must never dry out completely.
Feed Every two weeks, spring to early autumn.
Pot-on Every spring in a loam-based compost.
Propagation Divide in spring.

PROBLEM

Is the plant weak and spindly; are the leaflets turning yellow and dropping? Does the compost feel dry?

IF YES

CAUSE The plant has simply been kept very short of water.
ACTION Cut down all the stems to compost level, then water the plant thoroughly. New growth will soon make an appearance.

IF NO

Has the plant been in a hot room with direct sunlight.

IF YES

CAUSE Overheating.
ACTION Move the plant to a cooler room; keep it out of direct sunlight.

IF NO

Are there soft, light brown or hard, dark brown bumps on the stems and leaflets, especially on the undersides?

IF YES

CAUSE The bumps are scale insects, which suck the sap.
ACTION If there are only a few, scrape them off with a fingernail. If many, dose the compost with a systemic insecticide.

IF NO

Are the roots showing above the compost?

IF YES

CAUSE Asparagus ferns grow quickly and produce a mass of roots which start pushing the compost out of the pot. Eventually there is not enough compost left in the pot to hold all the water and food the plant needs to keep healthy.
ACTION Remove the entire plant to a larger pot with fresh compost, or divide the plant and repot both in separate pots in fresh compost.

OTHER SPECIES
Asparagus setaceus 'Nanus' has more delicate, feathery, rich green foliage.

PROBLEM

Are there brown patches on the leaves?

IF YES

CAUSE The plant has been exposed to direct sunlight and the leaves have been scorched.
ACTION Move the plant to a part of the room where it is out of the sun or to another room which gets little sun.

IF NO

When you push a finger into the compost does it feel sodden?

IF YES

CAUSE The plant has been watered too frequently and has probably been allowed to stand in water in its saucer. Overwatering can result in marked leaves and, in extreme cases, the roots may rot. Sodden compost prevents oxygen, vital for the plant's growth, from getting to the roots. Starved of oxygen, they begin to rot, and the plant is likely to die.
ACTION Let the compost dry out and then follow the watering instructions in **IDEAL CONDITIONS**. It is better to allow the compost to dry out almost completely between waterings.

IF NO

Have any of the leaves been touching a wall?

IF YES

CAUSE When the air is dry, wall plaster absorbs moisture from any source, inluding the leaves of plants which happen to be touching it. This results in brown patches on the leaves.
ACTION Move the plant a little way from the wall. Badly browned leaves should be removed completely.

PROBLEM

Does the plant appear to have stopped growing?

IF YES

CAUSE The plant has been languishing in a gloomy corner of the room. Aspidistras do not object to shade, but they still need an adequate level of light to produce new growth. Variegated aspidistras need more light than green-leaved, but not direct sunlight.
ACTION Move the plant closer to the window.

Aspidistra elatior
Aspidistras are native to China, Japan and the eastern Himalayas. Temperatures in summer may be 75°F/24°C, and in winter only 45°F/7°C. The plants are often found in shady mountain forests, and indoors they will tolerate more shade than most houseplants. The dark green leaves are lance-shaped and leathery.

IDEAL CONDITIONS

Temperature 60°F/16°C all year round, but the plant benefits from a winter rest at 50°F/10°C.
Light Shady position away from direct sun, but not in a dark corner.
Water Once or twice a week in spring and summer so that the compost is just moist all the time. In winter, once every 7 to 10 days, less frequently in low temperatures.
Feed Once a month in spring and summer.
Pot-on Once every three years in spring, in a loam-based compost.
Propagation Divide when potting-on.

Asplenium nidus
The asplenium is found in tropical rain forests of Australia, Africa and Asia. It is an epiphyte, growing on tree branches, but takes readily to life in a pot. The glossy, bright green lance-shaped fronds form a shuttlecock shape. In the wild, water and nutrients trickle down the fronds to the base of the rosette.

IDEAL CONDITIONS

Temperature All year at 65-70°F/ 18-21°C.
Light Bright, but it tolerates a certain amount of shade. It should not be in direct sunlight.
Water Once or twice a week, especially if kept in high temperature, into the centre of the rosette.
Feed Monthly, from late spring to early autumn.
Pot-on In spring in a peat-based compost.
Propagation From spores on the undersides of the leaves. This is a long and often tricky process.

PROBLEM

Have the leaf edges turned brown and papery and are whole leaves starting to yellow?

IF YES

CAUSE The air is too dry.
ACTION Make the air around the plant more humid by standing the pot on a tray of wet pebbles or by surrounding it with moist peat. Regular spraying also helps, but use rainwater if mains water is hard, to avoid lime deposits on the leaves. If the plant appears to be in a really sorry state, cut off all the fronds at the base in spring. New growth comes in several weeks.

IF NO

Has the plant been near a sunny window?

IF YES

CAUSE Direct sun has scorched the leaves.
ACTION Move the plant away from the window to a spot where light is good but without direct sun.

IF NO

Are there soft, light brown or hard, dark brown bumps on the undersides of the fronds at the edges or along the main rib?

IF YES

CAUSE These are scale insects which suck sap from the leaves, producing yellow spots that later turn brown and papery.
ACTION Scrape them off with a fingernail if there are only a few. Otherwise spray with dimethoate.

IF NO

Are there small brown dots arranged in regular lines on the undersides of the leaves?

IF YES

CAUSE These are the spore cases, containing thousands of spores from which the fern reproduces itself.
ACTION None, unless you want to try to propagate from them – a prolonged and difficult business.

OTHER SPECIES
Asplenium bulbiferum, has graceful feathery fronds. *Asplenium nidus* is bold-leafed.

PROBLEM

Are the leaves turning brown at the edges and falling?

━━━━━━━━━ **IF YES** ━━━━━━━━━

CAUSE The plant is being kept in a room with too high a temperature.
ACTION Simply move the plant to a cooler part of the room or into a room with a lower temperature.

━━━━━━━━━ **IF NO** ━━━━━━━━━

Does the compost feel dry just below the surface?

━━━━━━━━━ **IF YES** ━━━━━━━━━

CAUSE The plant has not been getting enough water; this is most likely to happen in summer.
ACTION Water the compost and then follow the routine given in **IDEAL CONDITIONS**. It is important that the compost should be evenly moist at all times.

━━━━━━━━━ **IF NO** ━━━━━━━━━

Are there fine white webs on leaves and stems?

━━━━━━━━━ **IF YES** ━━━━━━━━━

CAUSE The plant has been attacked by red spider mites, which are encouraged by warmth and a dry atmosphere.
ACTION Spray with liquid derris and respray every few days if necessary. If the aucuba must be kept in a temperature higher than those recommended, red spider mites can be discouraged by maintaining a humid atmosphere; either stand the pot on a tray of wet pebbles or surround it with moist peat. Regular mist spraying also helps.

PROBLEM

Are the leaves losing their yellow variegations?

━━━━━━━━━ **IF YES** ━━━━━━━━━

CAUSE The plant has not been getting enough light.
ACTION Move it to a spot nearer the window, but not where it will be in direct sunlight. A plant with variegated leaves needs more light than one with all-green leaves. The coloured areas are short of chlorophyll, which helps to convert sunlight into food for the plant; the green areas must, therefore, make up the shortfall and need brighter light to enable them to do this successfully.

Aucuba japonica 'Variegata'
Aucuba is an evergreen shrub native to Japan. It is often found growing in shady mountain forests. Summers are warm, but in winter temperatures may fall below 45°F/7°C. The plant does not object to shady, or even draughty, spots but reacts badly to excessive heat. Shiny, serrated leaves are flecked with yellow. Red berries.

IDEAL CONDITIONS

Temperature In summer 55-60°F/ 13-16°C; in winter 45°F/7°C, but it will tolerate somewhat higher temperatures.
Light Bright for preference, but will stand partial shade.
Water Twice a week in summer to keep compost moist. Every 7 to 10 days in winter, but more frequently if the plant is in a warm room.
Feed Every two weeks from late spring to early autumn.
Pot-on In spring in loam-based compost.
Propagation By stem cuttings in late summer.

Beaucarnea recurvata
Beaucarnea is an odd-looking succulent native to Mexico. The large bulbous root, partly exposed above the surface of the compost, provides storage for water. This reserve is vital for the plant's survival, since rainfall is irregular in its natural habitat. Long, narrow drooping leaves grow in a rosette around the green-brown trunk.

IDEAL CONDITIONS

Temperature In summer up to 75°F/24°C; the warmer, the better. In winter, rest the plant at 45°F/7°C.
Light Bright, with direct sun.
Water Twice a week from late spring to early autumn, so the compost is always moist. In winter, every two to three weeks in a cool room; more often in a warm one.
Feed Once a month from late spring to early autumn.
Pot-on Every two to three years, in a mixture of loam, peat and sand.
Propagation Remove offsets from the base of the plant, or sow seed in spring.

PROBLEM

Are the leaves pale and limp?

IF YES

CAUSE Poor light. Beaucarneas require excellent light.
ACTION Move the plant close to a window where it will get very bright light with direct sun. It needs shade only from scorching sun.

IF NO

Is growth generally weak?

IF YES

CAUSE Lack of food.
ACTION Apply a liquid feed to the compost once a month between late spring and early autumn.

IF NO

Does the compost feel dry below the surface when you push in a finger? Is the root shrivelling?

IF YES

CAUSE Underwatering – a sure sign is the shrivelling of the root, which serves as a water reservoir for the plant.
ACTION Water the plant, making sure that the compost is moist throughout. Let excess moisture drain away; the pot must not be left standing in water. Then follow watering instructions in **IDEAL CONDITIONS** taking care to adjust as indicated in winter.

IF NO

Does the compost feel wet just below the surface and is the bulbous root swollen?

IF YES

CAUSE Overwatering.
ACTION Let the compost dry out completely and do not water again until the root has reduced in size.

PROBLEM

Are the lower leaves falling?

IF YES

CAUSE This is the natural growth of the plant. As it matures, lower leaves fall and a trunk begins to form.
ACTION None.

PROBLEM

Are the leaves turning brown and papery at the edges, and are they curling?

Begonia rex
This exotic-looking **begonia** originated in the tropical rain forests of Assam. There, spring and summer temperatures are 90°F/32°C, those in winter 60°F/16°C. From the original species, numerous cultivars with striking leaf colours and textures have been developed. Green leaves have pink, red, purple, silver or mixed markings.

IF YES

CAUSE The plant has been kept in a hot, dry room.
ACTION Move the plant to a cooler room. Water the compost, and from then on provide a more humid atmosphere around the plant – either stand the pot on a tray of wet pebbles or surround it with moist peat.

IF NO

Are there fine white webs on leaves and stems?

IF YES

CAUSE Dry air has encouraged infestation by red spider mites.
ACTION Spray with liquid derris and repeat a few days later if necessary. A humid atmosphere will help to keep red spider mites away.

PROBLEM

Are the leaves falling in winter?

IF YES

CAUSE It is too cold for the plant.
ACTION Move the plant to a warmer room where the minimum temperature is 55°F/13°C.

IF NO

Are the stems and crown of the plant rotting?

IF YES

CAUSE Either the plant has been watered too often or the atmosphere is excessively humid.
ACTION If all the stems are affected, throw the plant away. Otherwise remove the affected stems and dust the compost with a fungicide powder. Allow the compost to dry out and then water as in **IDEAL CONDITIONS**.

IF NO

Are the leaves also covered with fluffy grey mould?

IF YES

CAUSE This is a fungal disease called *botrytis*, which is encouraged by excessive watering and humidity.
ACTION Spray with benomyl. Allow the compost to dry out and move the plant to a more airy spot.

IDEAL CONDITIONS

Temperature In summer 65-70°F/18-21°C; in winter 55-60°F/13-16°C.
Light Bright, but with no direct sun.
Water Twice a week in summer so that the compost is moist all the time. Every 7 to 10 days in winter.
Feed Every two weeks from late spring to early autumn.
Pot-on In spring in a peat-based compost.
Propagation Take leaf cuttings in summer.

Begonia tuberhybrida
This tuberous begonia
is native to South
America, in particular
Brazil, which enjoys hot,
humid summers, up to
75°F/24°C, and not
much lower in winter.
Rainfall is plentiful year-
round. Leaves are long
and heart-shaped with
serrated edges. White,
yellow, orange and
crimson flowers are
borne from early
summer to early autumn.

IDEAL CONDITIONS

Temperature From
spring to early
autumn, 65-70°F/
18-21°C. Store
dormant tubers at
45°F/7°C.
Light Bright, but
shade from direct
sun.
Water Once or twice
a week, but let the
surface of the
compost dry out
between waterings.
Dormant tubers must
be stored completely
dry.
Feed Every two
weeks from spring to
early autumn.
Pot-on In spring in
peat-based compost.
Propagation Divide
the tuber in spring,
ensuring that each
piece has a growing
shoot.

PROBLEM

Are the leaf edges turning brown?

IF YES

CAUSE The air is too dry.
ACTION Increase humidity around the plant – advice is
given in the introduction, page 8.

PROBLEM

Are leaves and stems covered with white powder?

IF YES

CAUSE The plant has been kept too wet and poorly
ventilated, and this has encouraged mildew disease.
ACTION Remove all infected leaves and spray with
benomyl. Move the plant to a better ventilated spot.
Allow the compost to dry out and then follow the
watering instructions in IDEAL CONDITIONS.

PROBLEM

Do the leaves have yellow and brown damp patches?

IF YES

CAUSE Overwatering, poor ventilation and excessive
humidity have led to leaf spot disease.
ACTION Remove infected leaves and spray with
benomyl. Allow the compost to dry out before watering again as in IDEAL CONDITIONS; increase ventilation.

PROBLEM

Are the leaves, stems and compost covered with a
fluffy grey deposit?

IF YES

CAUSE Overwatering has led to an outbreak of
botrytis, or grey mould.
ACTION Treat as above for leaf spot disease.

PROBLEM

After flowering are the leaves turning yellow?

IF YES

CAUSE Entirely natural. Tuberous begonias die down
and then have a dormant period.
ACTION Stop watering. When all leaves have died, cut
away withered foliage, remove tubers and store *dry*
in peat or sand at 45°F/7°C until spring.

PROBLEM

Has the plant grown lanky and spindly?

IF YES

CAUSE Probably too high a temperature in winter, but poor winter light has the same effect.
ACTION Remove the plant to a room where the temperature is no higher than 60°F/16°C. Place it as close to a window as possible.

IF NO

Has the plant grown tall and leggy since it finished flowering?

IF YES

CAUSE Shrimp plants have a natural tendency to sprawl, with the stems growing to 24in/60cm.
ACTION Cut back the stems to within 6in/15cm of the compost when the bracts start to fade or wait until the spring to do so. Once new growth is well established, keep pinching out the growing tips to encourage bushy growth.

PROBLEM

Have the bracts started to turn pale and yellow?

IF YES

CAUSE Not enough light.
ACTION Move the plant closer to a window where it will get direct sunlight, but shade it from the hottest sun.

IF NO

Are there also yellow patches on the leaves?

IF YES

CAUSE The plant has been overwatered.
ACTION First allow the compost almost to dry out and then follow the watering routine in **IDEAL CONDITIONS**. Try to ensure that in spring and summer the compost is never allowed to become waterlogged, while during the plant's winter rest in a lower temperature it is barely moist but never totally dry.

OTHER SPECIES

Beloperone guttata lutea has attractive yellow bracts but is less frequently seen.

Beloperone guttata
Beloperone, the shrimp plant, comes from tropical rain forest areas of Mexico, where temperatures average 75°F/24°C all year. Rain is plentiful at all times. The oval leaves are mid-green and slightly shiny. The pinkish-brown, shrimp-shaped bracts will last for many months in the right conditions. White flowers off and on during the summer.

IDEAL CONDITIONS

Temperature 65°F/18°C, with a short winter rest at 60°F/16°C.
Light Bright, with direct sun; shield from scorching, midday sun.
Water Once or twice a week in summer; allow the top layer of compost to dry out before watering again. Once every two weeks in winter; never allow the compost to dry out completely.
Feed Every two weeks from late spring to early autumn.
Pot-on In spring, in either peat- or loam-based compost.
Propagation Take stem cuttings in spring.

Billbergia nutans
Billbergia is a terrestrial bromeliad. Unlike epiphytic bromeliads, which live on tree branches and rocks, it grows on the ground, forming thick clumps. In its native Brazil and Argentina it flourishes in constant warmth and rain. Long, arching, dark green leaves have a metallic sheen. May flower at any time of year.

IDEAL CONDITIONS

Temperature 60-65°F/16-18°C all year.
Light Bright, with direct sun for good leaf colour and successful flowering. Shade from scorching sun.
Water Once or twice a week, depending on how high the temperature is. Allow the surface of the compost to dry out between waterings.
Feed Monthly, from spring to early autumn.
Pot-on In spring, in a peat-based compost.
Propagation When potting-on, remove good-sized offsets with sufficient roots to support them.

PROBLEM

Are the tips of the leaves turning brown and papery?

IF YES

CAUSE The air is too dry. While billbergias do not mind the warmth of centrally heated rooms, the dryness of the air does affect them. This is most obvious if they are near a radiator, where the air is not only very warm but also exceedingly dry. The leaves of plants touching a wall may be similarly affected; wall plaster is absorbent and in dry rooms will draw moisture from any available source – in this instance, the plant.
ACTION Move the plant away from the radiator or wall if the leaves have been touching it. Regular mist spraying helps to prevent the plant from drying out.

IF NO

When you push a finger into the compost does it feel dry 1in/2.5cm or more below the surface?

IF YES

CAUSE Underwatering.
ACTION Water the compost well, letting excess water drain away before returning the pot to its saucer. Then water as in **IDEAL CONDITIONS**.

PROBLEM

Are the leaves dull and pale, and has the plant refused to flower?

IF YES

CAUSE Not enough light. The intensity of light in a room drops dramatically only 6ft/1.8 m from a window. Areas to the side of a window are usually well in the shade, but white-painted walls help to reflect light.
ACTION Move the plant closer to the window so that it receives direct light. If possible, give the billbergia a spell outdoors in summer, but not in scorching sun.

OTHER SPECIES

Billbergia 'Fantasia' has coppery leaves, with cream and pink markings; red bracts, blue flowers.
Billbergia venezuelana has dark green leaves, marked maroon and silver; pink bracts, green and white flowers.

PROBLEM

Are the fronds brown at the tips? Are they turning yellow, shrivelling and falling?

Blechnum gibbum
This large fern comes from New Caledonia in the western Pacific, where summers are hot and humid, with thundery rain in the evenings. Winters are also warm, but tend to be drier. The fern grows a rosette of shiny, light green fronds, divided into tapering leaflets. As the lower leaves die, a scaly palm-like trunk develops.

IF YES

CAUSE The air is too dry and warm, as it often is in centrally heated rooms in winter.
ACTION Move the plant to a cooler part of the room, as far as possible from a radiator, provided the light is still good. Increase humidity by standing the pot on a tray of wet pebbles or surrounding it with moist peat.

IF NO

When you push a finger into the compost does it feel dry just below the surface?

IF YES

CAUSE The plant is short of water; it is important that the compost is moist throughout.
ACTION Remove any badly affected or obviously dead fronds. Water the compost thoroughly and follow the watering routine in **IDEAL CONDITIONS**.

IF NO

Has the fern been standing in a sunny window?

IF YES

CAUSE Sun has scorched the leaves.
ACTION Move the plant out of the direct sunshine; blechnums need good light but not direct sun.

PROBLEM

Are there small brown dots, arranged in regular formation, on the undersides of the fronds?

IF YES

CAUSE Entirely natural. These are not pests, as they may seem at first glance, but spore cases containing the thousands of spores from which the fern reproduces itself.
ACTION None, unless you remove them to try your skill at propagation, a lengthy and tricky operation.

OTHER SPECIES

Blechnum brasiliense, whose new fronds have a coppery tinge but later turn bright green.

IDEAL CONDITIONS

Temperature
65-75°F/18-24°C. May be rested in winter at around 60°F/16°C.
Light Bright, but away from direct sun.
Water Twice a week in summer, so the compost is evenly moist. Water a plant resting at a lower temperature in winter about once a week.
Feed Every two weeks, late spring to early autumn.
Pot-on In spring in a peat-based compost or a mix of peat, loam and sand.
Propagation From spores on undersides of leaves. Offsets occasionally grow at the base of the main plant and can be detached.

**B
O
U
G
A
I
N
V
I
L
L
E
A**

Bougainvillea buttiana
Bougainvilleas come originally from Brazil, where the weather is warm to hot, and sunny, with rain all year. They have small oval leaves and large white, yellow, red, orange or purple bracts around small cream flowers from early spring to early autumn. The plant tends to sprawl and is best trained around a hoop of wire.

IDEAL CONDITIONS

Temperature In summer, 65-70°F/18-21°C. Rest the plant in winter at about 55°F/13°C, but not lower than 50°F/10°C.
Light Bright, with as much direct sun as possible.
Water Twice a week in summer; allow the compost almost to dry out before rewatering. In winter, every 7 to 10 days; the lower the temperature, the less water is needed.
Feed Every two weeks, late spring to early autumn.
Pot-on In spring in a loam-based compost.
Propagation Take cuttings in spring; bottom heat of 75°F/24°C needed.

PROBLEM

Has the plant refused to flower? Are leaves falling?

IF YES

CAUSE Poor light. Bougainvilleas must have bright light with direct sun if they are to flower well. They do best in a conservatory or garden room. If the leaves fall in winter, there is no need to worry.
ACTION If possible, move the plant to a windowsill where it will have several hours of direct sunshine.

PROBLEM

Has the foliage turned yellow and is growth poor?

IF YES

CAUSE Underfeeding. Fresh compost contains nutrients which the plant uses up in about three months. Thereafter it must be given fertilizer.
ACTION Feed plants regularly every two weeks between late spring and early autumn.

IF NO

Does the compost feel wet just below the surface when you push in a finger?

IF YES

CAUSE Overwatering.
ACTION Let the compost almost dry out and then follow watering instructions in **IDEAL CONDITIONS**.

PROBLEM

Are the stems growing so long that the plant is getting out of hand?

IF YES

CAUSE This is the way it grows naturally.
ACTION The size of the plant can be restricted by pruning, which will also make it grow more bushy. In late winter, prune back the main stems to about one-third of their length, making cuts just above a leaf. Side shoots should be cut back to within 1in/2.5cm of the main stems.

OTHER SPECIES

Bougainvillea glabra, a climber, with bright green leaves, purple bracts, yellow flowers.

PROBLEM

Are the leaves and flowers covered in brown patches, and are the flowers falling?

IF YES

CAUSE Too much sunlight. Both flowers and leaves have been scorched.
ACTION Move the plant out of the direct line of the sun. Browallias do best in bright reflected light. They should have only two hours of weak sun a day.

IF NO

Has the plant been in a hot room, especially in winter?

IF YES

CAUSE Excessive heat. Browallia flowers will drop if the temperature rises above 65°F/18°C.
ACTION Move the plant to a cooler room. The ideal temperature range is 50-60°F/10-16°C.

PROBLEM

Have the stems become lanky, and has the plant stopped producing flowers?

IF YES

CAUSE The growing tips of the stems have not been pinched out nor faded flowers removed.
ACTION At intervals of three to four weeks, the growing tips of the stems should be pinched out to encourage bushy growth. As soon as flowers begin to fade, pick them off; this will encourage new buds to form.

PROBLEM

Are there green or black flies clinging to the stems and undersides of the leaves?

IF YES

CAUSE These are aphids, which suck sap, so weakening the plant and distorting leaves and flowers.
ACTION Spray with pyrethrum. Repeat the spraying every four days until all the aphids have disappeared. Keep a close watch to see that they do not return: deal with them before they get established.

OTHER SPECIES

Browallia speciosa 'Silver Bells': white flowers.
Browallia vicosa 'Sapphire': bright violet flowers.

Browallia speciosa 'Major'

Browallia is native to Colombia, in South America, where the temperature all year averages 60°F/16°C, and is seldom above 70°F/21°C. Rain falls year round, mostly in spring and autumn. The bright green leaves are slender and pointed. Large, blue-violet tubular flowers are produced from mid-summer to winter.

IDEAL CONDITIONS

Temperature Plants do well at 50-60°F/10-16°C but flower less well in warmer rooms in winter.
Light Bright, with reflected light or direct sunlight if not too fierce.
Water Twice a week; allow the surface of the compost to dry out between waterings.
Feed Every two weeks after flower buds appear until flowering is over.
Pot-on No. The plant is an annual and is discarded after flowering.
Propagation Sow seed in late winter and early spring for summer flowers; in late summer for winter flowers.

Brunfelsia calycina
Brunfelsia is an evergreen shrub, native to the tropical rain forests of Brazil. Average temperature is 80°F/26°C, and there is rain all year. The narrow, pointed leaves are leathery and shiny, but the interesting feature of the plant is the large flowers, from early summer to autumn. They open purple and fade to lavender to white within a few days.

IDEAL CONDITIONS

Temperature All year at 60-70°F/16-21°C, but if the plant stops flowering it can be rested for a few weeks at around 55°F/13°C.
Light Bright with some sun, but not fierce.
Water Twice a week to ensure compost is always moist. Resting plants need watering once a week at most.
Feed Every two weeks, late spring to early autumn.
Pot-on Every two or three years in a mixture of peat-based compost and leaf-mould.
Propagation Take stem cuttings in spring. Heat of 70°F/21°C is needed for cuttings to root.

PROBLEM

Are leaf tips turning brown, and has the plant refused to flower?

IF YES

CAUSE Air too dry and a fluctuating temperature.
ACTION Create a humid atmosphere around the plant by standing the pot on a tray of wet pebbles or by surrounding it with moist peat. The plant should be kept in a stable temperature of 60-70°F/16-21°C.

IF NO

Is the plant in a shaded part of the room?

IF YES

CAUSE Lack of light, and sunlight in particular. Brunfelsia will not flower if it does not have good light with some direct sun.
ACTION Move the plant close to a sunny window, shading it only from the hottest sun.

PROBLEM

Has the plant developed lanky growth with bare lower stems?

IF YES

CAUSE Older plants naturally grow like this.
ACTION In spring, cut down the stems to half their length. When new shoots appear, pinch out the tips regularly to encourage bushiness.

PROBLEM

Are there green or black flies on the undersides of leaves and clustering around the stems?

IF YES

CAUSE The plant has been attacked by aphids, as are many plants with soft, tender growth. Although aphids are a greater pest outdoors, they do operate indoors, especially if the air is dry.
ACTION Spray with pyrethrum. Repeat every few days while the aphids persist. Increase humidity as recommended above.

OTHER SPECIES
Brunfelsia calycina 'Macrantha' has large purple flowers with white eyes – very striking.

PROBLEM

Are the leaves turning brown at the edges and shrivelling?

IF YES

CAUSE The air has been too dry; one of the plant's major needs is adequate humidity.
ACTION Create humidity around the plant; see page 8.

IF NO

Has the plant been placed near an open door or a door which is frequently opened?

IF YES

CAUSE The plant has been in a draught.
ACTION Move it to a draught-free part of the room.

IF NO

Has the plant been in a cold room?

IF YES

CAUSE The temperature has fallen below the acceptable minimum for a caladium.
ACTION See IDEAL CONDITIONS for correct temperatures.

PROBLEM

Is the leaf colour paling?

IF YES

CAUSE Poor light.
ACTION Move the plant closer to a window, but not into direct sun; the thin leaves are easily scorched.

PROBLEM

Have the leaves started to die down in late summer?

IF YES

CAUSE Entirely natural. This marks the onset of the plant's dormant period.
ACTION Reduce the frequency of watering. When all the leaves have completely died down, cut them away. Store the tubers in the compost at a temperature of 60°F/16°C. During the period of dormancy, the compost should be only slightly moist. In early spring, remove the tubers from the old compost and repot in fresh. Water thoroughly and bring the pot into a temperature of 70°F/21°C. New growth should appear after a few weeks.

Caladium hortulanum
Caladiums come from tropical South America, in particular the hot, steamy jungles of Brazil. Temperatures average 80°F/26°C and rainfall is 100in/250cm all year. Paper-thin arrowhead leaves grow from tubers which have a dormant period in winter. Vivid combinations of leaf colour – green/white, red/green and white/red – are found.

IDEAL CONDITIONS

Temperature During the growing period, in the range 65-75°F/18-24°C. Store dormant tubers at 60°F/16°C.
Light Bright, but shade from direct sun.
Water Twice a week when in full growth so that the compost is always moist. Reduce watering when leaves begin to die down. Water dormant tubers about once a month.
Feed Every two weeks from the time leaves appear until they die down.
Pot-on In spring in a peat-based compost.
Propagation Detach newly produced tubers when potting-on the old plant.

Calathea makoyana
Calatheas come from the tropical rain forest areas of Brazil, especially in the south. Temperatures are around 80°F/26°C all year and rain is plentiful. Like caladiums, they have highly coloured foliage – broad, oval green leaves with darker leaf patterns and silvery markings. But, unlike caladiums, they do not die down in winter.

IDEAL CONDITIONS

Temperature
60-70°F/16-21°C all year, certainly no lower than 60°F/16°C.
Light Slightly shaded, but do not keep in gloomy corners.
Water Twice a week in summer so that the compost stays moist all the time. About once a week in winter; allow the surface to dry out between waterings. Use soft, lukewarm water.
Feed Every two weeks from late spring to early autumn.
Pot-on In early summer in peat-based compost.
Propagation Divide when potting-on.

PROBLEM

Have the edges of the leaves turned brown and papery? Are the leaves curling and turning yellow?

IF YES

CAUSE The air is too dry.
ACTION Increase humidity around the plant – stand the pot on a tray of wet pebbles or surround it with peat which is always kept moist. Mist spray the plant daily, using rainwater in hard-water areas to avoid marking the leaves.

IF NO

Are there also fine white webs on the leaves and stems and yellow spots on the leaves?

IF YES

CAUSE This is the work of sap-sucking red spider mites, attracted by the dryness of the air.
ACTION Spray with liquid derris every few days while the pests persist. Increase humidity, as above.

IF NO

When you push a finger into the compost does it feel dry just below the surface?

IF YES

CAUSE The plant is not getting enough water.
ACTION Water the compost thoroughly. During the active growth period, it should be moist always but not sodden.

PROBLEM

Are there brown patches on the leaves, and are they turning pale?

IF YES

CAUSE Too much light and direct sun.
ACTION Move the plant out of the line of the sun. Calatheas prefer a slightly shaded spot and should not be exposed to direct sun.

OTHER SPECIES

Calathea insignis has lance-shaped, light green leaves with olive markings, purple undersides. *Calathea picturata* has green-edged leaves with silvery grey centres.

PROBLEM

Are the leaves paling and reverting to plain green, and are the stems becoming straggly and bare?

IF YES

CAUSE Poor light. Plants with variegated leaves must have good light to maintain strong colouring. Spindly growth is also the result of poor light.
ACTION Move the plant near to a sunny window where it will get two to three hours of sunlight a day. Shade from very hot sun, however.

IF NO

Is the plant in its second year of growth?

IF YES

CAUSE As the callisia ages, it is natural that it should start to lose the lower leaves on its stems.
ACTION Cut back bare stems to compost level in spring; this will encourage new growth. But callisias are worth keeping for two years at the most. After that it is best to start a new plant from cuttings and throw the old one away.

IF NO

If the plant is in active growth, does the compost feel dry just below the surface when you stick in a finger?

IF YES

CAUSE Underwatering. Callisias are often grown in hanging containers to show off the foliage effectively. But hanging plants are at greater risk of being underwatered – the air is warmer higher in the room, and a container above eye level is often forgotten when other plants, more easily reached, are being watered. The ideal solution is to have the container on a chain and pulley so you can easily lower it to check the compost; do this daily in hot weather.
ACTION Remove any bare, spindly stems and water the compost thoroughly. Then follow the routine of watering in **IDEAL CONDITIONS**.

PROBLEM

Are the leaf tips turning brown at the edges?

IF YES

CAUSE The air is too dry.
ACTION Remove dying leaves; mist spray daily.

Callisia elegans
Callisias originate in the rain forests of Mexico, where temperatures average 75°F/24°C all year, with plenty of rain; there is no dry season. They are related to tradescantias and have the same creeping habit. Their trailing stems of dark green leaves with white stripes and purple undersides look best in a hanging container.

IDEAL CONDITIONS

Temperature In summer, 60-65°F/16-18°C. A few weeks' rest in winter at about 55°F/13°C benefits the plant.
Light Bright with direct sunlight, but shade from fierce sun.
Water Twice a week in summer, for the compost must always be moist. If the plant is kept in winter at a lower temperature, water once a week and allow the top layer of the compost to dry out between waterings.
Feed Every two weeks, late spring to early autumn.
Pot-on In spring in peat- or loam-based compost.
Propagation Stem tip cuttings in spring.

CAMPANULA

Campanula isophylla 'Mayi'
Campanulas are native to northern Italy, where summers are dry and warm, around 65°F/18°C, and winters 45-50°F/7-10°C. The small, heart-shaped leaves are pale grey-green; blue, star-like flowers are borne from late summer to early autumn. After flowering, the plant has a dormant period. Plants look best in hanging containers.

IDEAL CONDITIONS

Temperature The ideal range in spring and summer is only 45-55°F/7-13°C, but temperatures will, obviously, often be higher. Rest plants in winter at 45°F/7°C. Keep free from frost.
Light Bright, with a little direct sun. Do not expose to full sunlight.
Water Two or three times a week in summer; daily in hot weather. Seldom in winter.
Feed Every two weeks from late spring to early summer.
Pot-on In spring in a loam-based compost.
Propagation Take stem cuttings in spring.

PROBLEM

Are the flowers falling soon after they open?

IF YES

CAUSE The temperature is too high.
ACTION Move the plant to a cooler room where the temperature is around 55°F/13°C. If this is not possible, increasing humidity around the plant will help to prolong the life of the flowers. If the plant is not in a hanging container, stand the pot on a tray of wet pebbles or surround it with moist peat. Avoid mist spraying, since the flowers are easily damaged.

PROBLEM

Are the stems growing lanky, and is the plant refusing to flower?

IF YES

CAUSE Again, the room is too warm.
ACTION Move the plant to a cooler, well-ventilated spot. If possible, give it some time out of doors in summer but bring it in before there is any danger of ground frost. Cut back overlong stems and pinch out growing tips regularly to make the plant bushier.

IF NO

Is the plant in a shady position away from a window?

IF YES

CAUSE Poor light. Campanulas need bright light with some direct sunlight for sturdy growth and vigorous flowering.
ACTION Move the plant close to the window, but shade it from scorching sun.

PROBLEM

Has the plant started to die down after flowering?

IF YES

CAUSE Entirely natural; campanulas do this.
ACTION Cut back the stems to within 2in/5cm of the compost and give the plant a winter rest at 45°F/7°C, in good light. It will put out new growth in spring.

OTHER SPECIES
Campanula isophylla 'Alba' has white flowers.

PROBLEM

Has the fruit started to fall soon after forming?

─── **IF YES** ───

CAUSE The temperature is too high. Capsicums are often sold already in fruit in late autumn or early winter and at that time of the year, especially in a centrally heated house, it may be difficult to find a place cool enough for the plant.

ACTION Move it to a cooler room, or at least as far as possible from a radiator. The ideal temperature is about 55°F/13°C; above that, increasing humidity around the plant will help. Stand the pot on a tray of wet pebbles or surround it with moist peat. Spray daily.

─── **IF NO** ───

Are there fine white webs on the leaves or stems, or are there black and green insects on the undersides of the leaves?

─── **IF YES** ───

CAUSE The webs are a sign of an attack by red spider mites and the insects are aphids – both encouraged by a dry atmosphere.

ACTION If red spider mites, spray with liquid derris; if aphids, with pyrethrum. More than one application may be needed. Maintain a humid atmosphere.

─── **IF NO** ───

Is the plant in a shady part of the room?

─── **IF YES** ───

CAUSE Fruit will fall rapidly if there is not enough light, especially in the short hours of winter daylight.

ACTION Move the plant to a well-lit windowsill or as close as possible to a window.

─── **PROBLEM** ───

Are the leaves turning yellow? Does the compost feel dry just below the surface?

─── **IF YES** ───

CAUSE The compost is far too dry.

ACTION Remove the affected leaves. Water the compost thoroughly – until water runs out of the drainage hole in the bottom of the pot. Thereafter, follow the watering instructions in **IDEAL CONDITIONS**.

Capsicum annuum
The home of the chili pepper is high ground in Mexico, where humidity is high and the average temperature 60°F/16°C. Leaves are lance-shaped, and white flowers from early summer to early autumn are followed by orange and red fruits shaped like cones, fingers or cherries. After fruits fall, the plant is usually discarded.

IDEAL CONDITIONS

Temperature In summer, 55-65°F/ 13-18°C. Around 55°F/13°C in winter.
Light Bright, with direct sun, but shade from scorching sun.
Water Twice a week in summer so that the compost is always moist. Once a week should be enough in winter, especially if the plant is kept at a low temperature.
Feed Weekly after the flowers appear until fruit begins to form.
Pot-on Not necessary.
Propagation Sow seed in spring; maintain a temperature of 65°F/18°C.

Cattleya bowringiana
This epiphytic orchid, found growing on trees or rocky outcrops in its native Honduras, thrives in the warm, humid conditions of the tropical rain forest. Average temperature is 75°F/24°C, and there is rain throughout the year. Each pseudobulb has a pair of strap-shaped leaves and purple flowers, with darker lips, in autumn.

IDEAL CONDITIONS

Temperature By day, always 65-75°F/ 18-24°C; slightly lower at night, but not below 60°F/16°C.
Light Bright, but not direct sunlight.
Water Two or three times a week in summer so that the compost is constantly moist. Once a week in winter, letting the compost almost dry out before watering again. Needs a humid atmosphere.
Feed Monthly, from spring to early autumn.
Pot-on Every two or three years in spring in a special compost for orchids.
Propagation By division of the rhizome when repotting.

PROBLEM

Has the plant refused to flower?

IF YES

CAUSE The temperature is too low.
ACTION Maintain an even temperature of 65-75°F/18-24°C by day all year round; a few degrees lower at night.

IF NO

Are the leaf tips turning brown and does the air feel very dry?

IF YES

CAUSE The orchid is suffering from a lack of humidity.
ACTION Stand the pot on a tray of wet pebbles or place the pot within a large container filled with moist peat.

IF NO

Is the plant in a shady part of the room?

IF YES

CAUSE There is not enough light; cattleyas will not flower if they are kept in a poor light.
ACTION Move the plant close to a window, but not into direct sunlight, which can scorch the leaves.

IF NO

Are the pseudobulbs beginning to shrivel?

IF YES

CAUSE They are not being given sufficient water.
ACTION Water the plant thoroughly until excess water runs out of the drainage hole in the pot. Then follow the watering instructions in **IDEAL CONDITIONS**. In summer, the compost should be moist always, but in winter it should be allowed almost to dry out between waterings.

IF NO

Are there both soft and hard brown lumps on the lower part of the pseudobulbs?

IF YES

CAUSE The orchid has been attacked by scale insects.
ACTION If there are only a few, scrape them off with a fingernail. In heavy infestations, spray with malathion.

◇ **PROBLEM** ◇

Have the hairs on the cactus changed from silvery white to dull grey, and is the column going bald from the base upward?

═══ IF YES ═══

CAUSE This is what happens to a cephalocereus as it grows old.
ACTION Nothing can be done. However, if the hairs on a young plant lose colour, they are probably matted with dirt. Wash them carefully with soapy water, using a soft brush, and wash away all soap afterwards. This is best done on a warm, drying day. You can avoid the need to wash the hairs by regularly brushing them very gently with a soft brush.

─── PROBLEM ───

Has the stem started to elongate? Is growth mishapen?

═══ IF YES ═══

CAUSE Too little light, especially in winter.
ACTION Move the cactus to a windowsill where it will get plenty of sun.

═══ IF NO ═══

Has the plant been kept in normal room temperatures during the winter months?

═══ IF YES ═══

CAUSE It has been too warm.
ACTION See **IDEAL CONDITIONS**.

═══ IF NO ═══

Are there white woolly areas on the surface of the stem? (These may be difficult to detect.)

═══ IF YES ═══

CAUSE Mealy bugs, which suck the sap and leave unsightly yellow patches.
ACTION Spray with liquid derris or pyrethrum. Repeat the spraying every few days while the pests persist.

─── PROBLEM ───

Has the cactus started to rot at its base?

═══ IF YES ═══

CAUSE Too frequent watering, especially when the plant is being rested in winter at a low temperature.
ACTION Start again with another plant.

Cephalocereus senilis
This cactus is native to hot, arid and windy areas of Mexico. By day, the temperature may be 100°F/38°C; at night, ground frost is possible. Rainfall is low, in short sharp cloudbursts. The fleshy, columnar stem of the cactus is covered with white hairs, which give some protection in its adverse natural environment. Seldom flowers indoors.

IDEAL CONDITIONS

Temperature During the summer will tolerate any amount of heat. In winter, the cactus should be rested at about 50°F/10°C, but not lower than 45°F/7°C.
Light Full sun all year round.
Water Twice a week in summer, to keep the compost moist but never sodden. Once a week in winter should be enough.
Feed Every two weeks from late spring to early autumn.
Pot-on In spring, in a mix of loam- and peat-based compost with one-third sand.
Propagation Sow seed in spring.

Chamaedorea elegans
The chamaedorea is a palm from tropical rain forest areas of Mexico, which have an average temperature of 70°F/21°C and rainfall throughout the year. Since it does not grow very tall, it is overshadowed by other forest trees and will tolerate some shade in the home. The long yellow-green stems bear almost opposite pairs of narrow leaflets.

IDEAL CONDITIONS

Temperature In summer, 65-70°F/18-21°C. Rest the palm in winter 55-60°F/13-16°C.
Light Slight shade but no dark corners.
Water Twice a week in summer, when the compost should be moist always. Once a week in winter: the compost should be just moist.
Feed Monthly, spring to early autumn.
Pot-on In spring, in peat-based compost with one-third sand added.
Propagation Sow seed in spring; bottom heat of 75°F/24°C is necessary. The plant takes a long time to grow to a reasonable size.

PROBLEM

Are the tips of the leaves turning brown?

IF YES

CAUSE The air is too dry.
ACTION Create humidity in the vicinity of the palm by standing the pot on a tray of wet pebbles or by placing it in a larger container, filled with peat that is kept constantly moist.

IF NO

Are there also white webs on the fronds and stems, with yellow patches on the leaflets?

IF YES

CAUSE The palm is being attacked by red spider mites, encouraged by dry air. They suck the sap and leave ugly marks on the fronds.
ACTION Spray with liquid derris. Repeat every few days until there is no sign of the mites. Increase humidity, as described, to keep the insects at bay.

PROBLEM

Is the palm's growth spindly?

IF YES

CAUSE Not enough light. This palm will tolerate a shady spot, but not a dark corner.
ACTION Move the plant closer to a window so that it gets plenty of light but no direct sun.

IF NO

Are the fronds also shrivelling and dying?

IF YES

CAUSE The palm is being kept too warm and has probably been in direct sun.
ACTION Move it to a cooler part of the room or to a cooler room altogether, especially during the winter rest period. While the palm will be all right if kept at 65-70°F/18-21°C in summer, during the winter rest period the temperature should be as low as 55-60°F/13-16°C. Always keep out of direct sunlight.

OTHER SPECIES
Chamaedorea seifrizii: reed-like stems.

PROBLEM

Does the palm seem slow in producing new fronds during the summer growth period?

IF YES

CAUSE It is not getting enough light.
ACTION Move the pot closer to a window, where the palm will get two to three hours of direct sun a day. Growth slows considerably in shade.

PROBLEM

Are the leaf tips turning brown?

IF YES

CAUSE Underwatering. During the summer months, the compost should be moist always but not sodden.
ACTION Thoroughly water the compost until excess water runs through the drainage hole in the pot. Thereafter, water as in **IDEAL CONDITIONS**.

IF NO

Are the leaves also curling and turning yellow?

IF YES

CAUSE Overwatering, which has rotted the roots and caused the plant to collapse. This is most likely to happen if the plant has been left standing in water in its saucer.
ACTION Remove the plant from the pot. Gently tease away the compost from the roots and cut away any obviously dead and soft roots. Repot in fresh compost to which liquid fungicide has been added, then follow watering instructions as in **IDEAL CONDITIONS**.

PROBLEM

Are emerging fronds covered with what looks like grey meal or hair?

IF YES

CAUSE This is a natural phase in the growth of the palm, not a disease, although it may look like one.
ACTION None needed, except to stop worrying. The film will soon fall off of its own accord.

OTHER SPECIES

Chamaerops humilis 'Elegans', with silvery instead of grey-green leaves.

Chamaerops humilis
The European fan plam is native to Europe, Spain and southern Italy in particular. There, average summer temperature is 65°F/18°C, falling in winter to 45-50°F/7-10°C. Far higher or lower temperatures are sometimes experienced. The fan-shaped fronds have deeply dissected, grey-green pointed segments.

IDEAL CONDITIONS

Temperature In summer, around 55°F/13°C, but the palm will tolerate higher temperatures. Give it a winter rest at about 45°F/7°C, but no lower than 40°F/4°C.
Light Bright, with some direct sun.
Water Twice a week in summer to keep the compost moist. Every 7 to 10 days in winter, especially in a low temperature.
Feed Every two weeks, late spring to early autumn.
Pot-on Every two or three years in spring, in a mix of two-thirds peat-based compost and one-third sand.
Propagation By removing suckers from the base.

**C
H
L
O
R
O
P
H
Y
T
U
M**

Chlorophytum comosum
'Vittatum'
The spider plant comes
from the grasslands of
South Africa. Summer
temperatures are
65-80°F/18-27°C; in
winter they can be low,
often with frost. The
arching leaves are pale
green, with a cream
streak down the centre.
Small white flowers in
spring and summer are
followed by plantlets on
runners. Looks best in a
hanging container.

IDEAL CONDITIONS

Temperature Normal
room temperatures
all year. The plant
will withstand cool
conditions, but not
below 45°F/7°C.
Light Bright, some
direct (not fierce) sun.
Water Two or three
times a week in
summer to keep
compost moist. Once
a week in winter; let
the surface dry out
between waterings.
Feed Every two
weeks from spring to
early autumn.
Pot-on In spring in
loam-based compost.
Propagation From
the plantlets at the
end of a runner. Pin
them down in pots of
compost until they
root well, then cut the
runners away from
the parent plant.

PROBLEM

Are the tips of the leaves turning brown?

IF YES

CAUSE Underwatering is usually the cause of this
common problem.
ACTION Water the compost well, until water is running
through the drainage hole in the pot. Then water as in
IDEAL CONDITIONS, ensuring that the compost is always
moist in summer. The browned tips of the leaves can
be cut away, but do not cut into the green part of the
leaf or the browning will soon spread.

IF NO

Has the plant been in a sunny window?

IF YES

CAUSE The sun has scorched the leaves.
ACTION Move the plant away from the window, out of
the line of the sun. Chlorophytums enjoy some sun but
must not be exposed to fierce sunlight.

PROBLEM

Are the leaves losing their contrasting creamy-white
markings?

IF YES

CAUSE Not enough light.
ACTION Move the plant to another part of the room,
where the light is brighter. Colour will soon return.

PROBLEM

Is growth lanky, with leaves shrivelling and dying?

IF YES

CAUSE The air is too hot and the compost too dry.
ACTION Move the plant to a cooler spot in the room or
to a cooler room. Keep the compost moist.

IF NO

Are the leaves also rotting at their base?

IF YES

CAUSE Overwatering; the compost has become waterlogged and the result is crown rot.
ACTION Let the compost dry out and hope that the plant
will recover, but you may well lose it.

PROBLEM

Are the tips of the leaves turning brown?

─────── **IF YES** ───────

CAUSE The air is too dry; a common problem with palms.
ACTION Create a humid atmosphere around the plant: see advice on page 8.

─────── **IF NO** ───────

If you push a finger into the compost, does it feel dry just below the surface?

─────── **IF YES** ───────

CAUSE The compost has been allowed to dry out.
ACTION Water it thoroughly until water runs out of the drainage hole in the pot; this ensures that the compost is wet right through. In future, follow the watering instructions in **IDEAL CONDITIONS**; the compost should always be moist but not sodden.

─────── **IF NO** ───────

As well as the browning of the leaf tips are there brown marks on the leaflets?

─────── **IF YES** ───────

CAUSE The leaves have been scorched by hot sun.
ACTION Move the palm out of the direct line of the sun or shade it when the sun is fiercest.

─────── **IF NO** ───────

Do the brown marks feel damp?

─────── **IF YES** ───────

CAUSE The plant has leaf spot disease; this is usually a sign of overwatering, excessive humidity and poor ventilation.
ACTION Remove affected leaflets and complete fronds if necessary. Spray with benomyl and repeat every few days if the condition persists. Allow the compost to dry out then water as in **IDEAL CONDITIONS**. Increase ventilation; in summer, a spell outdoors will benefit the palm, but a sudden change would be damaging. Light outdoors is far more intense than that indoors, so acclimatize the palm gradually over a period of a week or so by leaving it out for a longer time each day. Choose a sheltered spot.

Chrysalidocarpus lutescens
This elegant palm is a native of Mauritius, where it thrives in humid heat. Average temperature is 75°F/ 24°C all year. Rain falls mainly in summer, often in thundery showers. Yellow, arching stems carry almost opposite pairs of yellow-green leaves. The palm needs warmth and humidity to do well and, eventually, room to spread.

IDEAL CONDITIONS

Temperature 65-75°F/18-24°C all year. The palm may be rested at 60°F/16°C, but no lower.
Light Bright with direct, but not fierce, sun.
Water Twice a week all year, but plants resting in winter at lower temperatures need less frequent watering. Needs a humid atmosphere.
Feed Monthly, spring to early autumn.
Pot-on In spring in a mixture of peat and loam.
Propagation Remove suckers from the base of the plant when potting-on. Sow seed in spring; it is slow to germinate, so patience is needed.

Cissus antarctica
The kangaroo vine is native to Australia, particularly the temperate forest areas of Queensland's coast where summers are warm, 70°F/21°C, and winters mild, 55°F/13°C. Rainfall is even all year. Shiny, leathery leaves, with serrated edges, open light green and turn dark green as they mature. The vine can be allowed to trail or trained to climb.

IDEAL CONDITIONS

Temperature In summer, 55-65°F/ 13-18°C. Rest the plant at about 55°F/13°C in winter, but the temperature must not fall below 50°C/10°C.
Light Bright, but shade from direct sun.
Water Twice a week in summer so that the compost is always moist. Once every 10 to 14 days in winter.
Feed Every two weeks, late spring to early autumn.
Pot-on In spring in a mixture of loam, peat, leaf-mould and sand.
Propagation Sow seed in spring. Take stem cuttings in spring and summer. Bottom heat of 75°F/ 24°C is required.

PROBLEM

Are there brown marks on the leaves? Before they started turning brown did they look transparent?

IF YES

CAUSE The plant has been exposed to direct sunlight.
ACTION Move the plant out of the line of the sun and in future always shade it. Remove any badly browned leaves.

IF NO

Is the atmosphere in the room warm and dry?

IF YES

CAUSE Lack of humidity.
ACTION Mist spray the plant daily during very warm, dry weather.

IF NO

Are the leaves turning yellow and falling? Does the compost feel wet just below the surface?

IF YES

CAUSE The compost has become too wet. This is likely to happen if the pot has been left standing in water in its saucer.
ACTION Empty the saucer and allow the compost to dry out a little before watering again. Then follow the watering routine in **IDEAL CONDITIONS**.

IF NO

Are there fine white webs on the leaves and stems?

IF YES

CAUSE The plant has been attacked by red spider mites, encouraged by the dry air.
ACTION Spray with liquid derris and create a humid atmosphere to keep the insects away by mist spraying the plant daily.

PROBLEM

Have the lower leaves fallen from the stems?

IF YES

CAUSE This is, unfortunately, natural.
ACTION In spring, any bare stems should be cut down to 4in/10cm. Once there is strong new growth, pinch out growing tips to encourage bushiness.

PROBLEM

Has the plant produced little or no fruit?

IF YES

CAUSE The flowers have not been pollinated.
ACTION Nothing can be done in the current year. In future, put the plant outdoors in summer so that insects can do the job of pollination. If the plant has to be kept indoors, draw a soft paintbrush over the blooms to spread the pollen.

IF NO

Is the plant in a shady part of the room?

IF YES

CAUSE Not enough sunlight. Citrus plants need good light and sun for successful flowering and fruiting.
ACTION Move to a window where the plant can get sun all year round.

PROBLEM

Are the leaves falling?

IF YES

CAUSE The air is too dry.
ACTION To raise the level of humidity around the plant, put the pot on a tray of wet pebbles or stand it in a container of moist peat.

IF NO

Are there also fine white webs on leaves and stems?

IF YES

CAUSE The presence of red spider mites, encouraged by the dryness of the air.
ACTION Spray with liquid derris, repeating every few days if the mites persist, and remove badly affected leaves. Maintain a humid atmosphere.

PROBLEM

Is the plant getting out of hand and losing its shape?

IF YES

CAUSE This is entirely natural for a citrus, but it can be tidied up.
ACTION In spring, cut back any overlong stems, then regularly pinch out growing tips for bushy growth.

Citrus mitis
This miniature orange tree is a native of tropical forests in the Philippines. The climate is warm (75°F/24°C average) and moist, with most rain falling from spring to autumn. Glossy oval leaves; white fragrant flowers in summer are followed by green fruits, turning orange. Given the right care, the fruit stays on the plant for many weeks.

IDEAL CONDITIONS

Temperature In summer, 65°F/18°C. Rest the plant in winter at around 55°F/13°C, never below 50°F/10°C.
Light Bright, with direct sun all year.
Water Twice a week in summer, keeping the compost always moist. Every 7 to 10 days in winter.
Feed Every two weeks from late spring to early autumn.
Pot-on Every other year in spring in loam-based compost with bonemeal added.
Propagation Sow seed in spring or take stem cuttings. Bottom heat of 70-75°F/21-24°C is required for both.

Clivia miniata
The Kaffir lily comes
from scrub areas of
South Africa, where
average temperature is
65°F/18°C in the dry
summers and 55°F/13°C
in the wet winters. In the
northern hemisphere,
water the plant well in
summer and keep it
fairly dry in winter to
encourage the orange
trumpet-shaped flower
to appear in late winter
or early spring.

IDEAL CONDITIONS

Temperature In
summer, 65°F/18°C.
Rest the plant for
about eight weeks
during winter at
50-55°F/10-13°C.
Water In summer,
twice a week so the
compost is always
moist. During the rest
period, once a month.
Light Bright with
some, but not
scorching, sun.
Feed Monthly, spring
to early autumn.
Pot-on Every two or
three years in loam-
based compost.
Propagation By
offsets which appear
at the base of the
plant. Remove them
only when they are a
good size and take
them with sufficient
roots to support the
new plant.

PROBLEM

Has the plant failed to flower in spring, or not
produced a flower spike at any time during the
year?

IF YES

CAUSE The plant has not had a winter rest period.
ACTION To encourage it to flower the following year,
move the clivia in autumn to a room in which the
temperature is 50-55°F/10-13°C, and leave it there for
about eight weeks. Even if the plant has been rested,
the flower spike may not appear until late spring or
early summer.

IF NO

Is there a flower head, with one or two flowers visible,
which is failing to push itself up between the leaves?

IF YES

CAUSE Again the plant has not had a proper rest.
ACTION Move it as close as possible to a window so that
the plant is exposed to bright light. This will encourage the flower head to emerge fully.

PROBLEM

After the flowers have fallen, are fruits beginning to
develop?

IF YES

CAUSE This is perfectly natural, but the plant should be
prevented from reaching this stage. The fruits contain
developing seed; if they remain on the plant, there is
less chance that the clivia will flower next year.
ACTION As soon as the last flower has fallen, cut off the
flower head only, leaving the stalk to wither away
naturally. Pull it away when it has shrivelled.

PROBLEM

Are there soft, light brown bumps or hard, dark
brown bumps on the undersides of the leaves,
especially at the edges?

IF YES

CAUSE The plant has been attacked by scale insects.
They suck the sap and make brown circles on the
leaves, permanently disfiguring them.
ACTION If there are only a few insects, scrape them off
with a fingernail; if many, spray with malathion.
Repeat the treatment every few days if necessary.

◇ PROBLEM ◇

Are the multicoloured leaves turning pale and reverting to plain green?

=== IF YES ===

CAUSE Insufficient light.
ACTION Move the plant close to a window, where it will get sun all year round.

=== PROBLEM ===

Are the edges of the leaves turning brown and are whole leaves falling?

=== IF YES ===

CAUSE The air is too dry.
ACTION Ensure humidity by following advice on page 8.

=== IF NO ===

Are the leaves and stems covered with white powder and fine white webs?

=== IF YES ===

CAUSE Red spider mites, which suck the sap.
ACTION Spray with liquid derris or malathion, repeating every few days while the insects persist. The mites flourish in dry air, whereas a humid atmosphere helps to deter them. Increase the humidity around the plant as described on page 8.

=== IF NO ===

Is the plant near an open door or one that is frequently open and closed?

=== IF YES ===

CAUSE The plant has been exposed to draughts and fluctuating temperatures, which cause leaves to drop.
ACTION Move the plant to a part of the room where there are no draughts. See **IDEAL CONDITIONS**.

=== IF NO ===

Has the plant become tall and leggy, and are the lower stems bare?

=== IF YES ===

CAUSE This is natural as the plant gets older.
ACTION To rejuvenate it, cut back the stems in early spring to within 6in/15cm of the compost. New growth will soon appear.

C
C
O
D
I
A
E
■
M

Codiaeum variegatum pictum
The croton is a native of Malaysia, thriving in hot (82°F/28°C), humid forests with rain all year. There is a wide variety of leaf shapes – broad, narrow, oblong, lobed – and colours – combinations of yellow, green, pink, brown, orange and black. Codiaeums must have warmth, excellent light, and humidity to stay looking good.

IDEAL CONDITIONS

Temperature
60-70°F/16-21°C all year, but they will tolerate a winter rest with a temperature no lower than 55°F/13°C.
Light Bright, with some direct sun for good leaf colour.
Water Twice a week in summer to keep the compost moist. Once a week in lower winter temperatures. Needs humid conditions.
Feed Every two weeks from late spring to early autumn.
Pot-on In spring in peat-based compost.
Propagation Take stem or basal cuttings in summer.

Coleus blumei
The flame nettle comes from Java, a country largely covered with tropical rain forest. The average temperature is high, 80°F/27°C, and rain falls throughout the year. The heart-shaped leaves have serrated edges and show colour combinations of green, brown, yellow, red and orange. The plants are perennial but soon become woody and large.

IDEAL CONDITIONS

Temperature
60-65°F/16-18°C all year. If the plant is kept during the winter, it will survive a temperature down to 55°F/13°C.
Light Bright, with direct sun. Shade only from fierce sun.
Water Two or three times a week in summer, more in very hot weather; once a week in winter.
Feed Every two weeks, late spring to early autumn.
Pot-on Every two to three months in the vigorous growing period in lime-free loam- or peat-based compost.
Propagation Take stem cuttings in late summer; they will root in water.

PROBLEM

Are the leaves wilting and dropping?

IF YES

CAUSE The temperature is too low.
ACTION Move the plant to a room where the temperature is 60-65°F/16-18°C. A coleus should never be kept in a temperature lower than 55°F/13°C.

IF NO

Is the atmosphere in the room hot and dry?

IF YES

CAUSE Lack of humidity.
ACTION Increase humidity around the plant by standing the pot on a tray of wet pebbles or by surrounding it with moist peat.

IF NO

Are there fine white webs on leaves and stems?

IF YES

CAUSE Red spider mites are present, encouraged by the dry air.
ACTION Spray with liquid derris or malathion, repeating the treatment every few days until the insects have been eliminated. Maintain a more humid atmosphere, as described above.

IF NO

When you push a finger into the compost is it dry just below the surface?

IF YES

CAUSE The plant is short of water.
ACTION Water the compost thoroughly and then follow the watering instructions in **IDEAL CONDITIONS**. In the growing period, the compost should be kept constantly moist.

PROBLEM

Are the leaves losing their colour?

IF YES

CAUSE Not enough light.
ACTION Move the plant close to a bright window with direct sunlight. Shade from fierce midday sun.

PROBLEM

Are the leaves turning brown and falling, and has the plant refused to flower?

══════════ IF YES ══════════

CAUSE The air is too dry.
ACTION Increase humidity. If the columnea is not in a hanging container, place the pot on a tray of wet pebbles or surround it with moist peat. If it is in a hanging container, mist spray the plant at least twice a day. Use rainwater if you live in a hard-water area, since lime marks the leaves.

══════════ IF NO ══════════

Is the plant in a shady part of the room?

══════════ IF YES ══════════

CAUSE Not enough light.
ACTION Move it to a place where it will get plenty of light, but out of direct sun. Columneas must have bright light at all times in order to flower.

══════════ IF NO ══════════

Has the plant been kept in a very warm room during the winter months?

══════════ IF YES ══════════

CAUSE Lack of a winter rest period may make a columnea reluctant to flower.
ACTION During the next winter, give it a period of rest at a lower temperature – around 60°F/13°C.

══════════ IF NO ══════════

As well as falling leaves and lack of flowers, are the stems rotting at the base?

══════════ IF YES ══════════

CAUSE Too much water has led to stem rot.
ACTION Allow the compost to dry out. Remove any badly affected stems and dust the compost with a fungicide powder. Follow the watering instructions in **IDEAL CONDITIONS**. In winter, water only occasionally; overwatering may inhibit flowering in the spring.

OTHER SPECIES
Columnea banksii has fleshy leaves and scarlet flowers.

Columnea microphylla
The goldfish vine is a trailing epiphyte that clings to trees, anchored by its roots. Its home is in the steamy rain forests of Costa Rica, with average heat of 75°F/24°C, and rain all year. Small dark green leaves grow on long stems, both covered with red hairs. Red-tipped flowers with yellow throats in spring. Looks best in a hanging basket.

IDEAL CONDITIONS

Temperature A steady 65°F/18°C in the growing period. Rest the plant in winter at 60°F/16°C.
Light Bright, but out of direct sunlight.
Water Once or twice a week in summer. The compost should be just moist; allow the surface to dry out between waterings. In winter, every 7 to 10 days to stop the compost drying out completely. Needs a humid atmosphere.
Feed Every two weeks, late spring to early autumn.
Pot-on Every other year after flowering, in a peat-based compost.
Propagation Take stem cuttings after flowering.

Cordyline terminalis
'Red Edge'
The cordyline is native to the tropical rain forests of Polynesia. Daytime temperature is 75°F/24°C, nights are a little cooler. Rain falls at all times of the year, with thundery showers almost daily in summer. Plants form rosettes of arching, bright green leaves edged, and often streaked, with red. They must have warmth and humidity.

IDEAL CONDITIONS

Temperature All year round at 70°F/21°C, but the plant can rest in winter at not lower than 60°F/16°C.
Light Bright, but shade from direct sun, which can scorch the leaves.
Water Once or twice a week in summer to keep the compost always moist. Once a week in winter if the plant is resting at a lower temperature.
Feed Every two weeks, late spring to early autumn.
Pot-on Every other year in spring in peat-based compost.
Propagation In spring, detach suckers thrown up from the base of the plant, or sow seed.

PROBLEM

Are the leaf edges turning brown, and are leaves falling?

IF YES

CAUSE The air is too dry for a plant which needs a humid, warm atmosphere.
ACTION The cordyline benefits greatly from being stood on a tray of wet pebbles or surrounded by moist peat; see advice on page 8.

IF NO

Does the compost feel dry just below the surface when you stick a finger in?

IF YES

CAUSE The compost has dried out too much as a result of infrequent watering.
ACTION Water the compost thoroughly so that water runs through the drainage hole in the pot. Keep the compost moist thereafter, following the watering instructions in **IDEAL CONDITIONS**.

IF NO

Do the leaves feel soft?

IF YES

CAUSE The temperature is too low.
ACTION Remove badly affected leaves. See **IDEAL CONDITIONS**.

IF NO

Are there brown marks all over the leaves?

IF YES

CAUSE The leaves have been scorched by the sun.
ACTION Move the plant out of the line of direct sun.

IF NO

Has the plant become leggy with bare stems?

IF YES

CAUSE As the plant gets older, the lower leaves fall naturally.
ACTION There is nothing that can be done to prevent this. Eventually the plant will begin to look ridiculous, but you can cut off the top and try to root it; bottom heat will be needed.

PROBLEM

Is the plant growing spindly, and are the leaves yellowing?

=== IF YES ===

CAUSE Not enough light.
ACTION Move the plant close to a sunny window, where it will get excellent light, with some direct sun; do not expose it to the hottest sun. In the wild, this crassula produces white flowers, turning to pink as they mature, but it is unlikely to flower indoors however much light it gets.

=== IF NO ===

Are there white fluffy balls on the stems and leaves?

=== IF YES ===

CAUSE The plant has been attacked by mealy bugs, which are cocooned inside these fluffy balls. The insects suck sap, causing the leaves to turn yellow and eventually fall.
ACTION Wash off the balls, scraping away any insects. Spray the plant with liquid derris or pyrethrum, repeating the treatment every few days until all the pests have been destroyed.

=== IF NO ===

Are the leaves wilting, and do they feel soft?

=== IF YES ===

CAUSE The plant has been overwatered, and the leaves have come bloated with the excess water. This is most likely to happen in winter.
ACTION Allow the compost almost to dry out and then follow the watering routine in **IDEAL CONDITIONS**.

=== PROBLEM ===

Are the leaves shrivelling?

=== IF YES ===

CAUSE Underwatering. This also is more likely to happen in winter.
ACTION Water the compost thoroughly and then water as in **IDEAL CONDITIONS**.

OTHER SPECIES
Crassula argentea has bright green, oval leaves.

Crassula aborescens
This succulent comes from Cape Province, South Africa, where temperatures range from 70°F/21°C in summer to 50°F/10°C in winter. Summer months are dry, rain falling mainly in winter. In the northern hemisphere, water the plant well in summer and keep it almost dry in winter. The small grey-green, red-edged fleshy leaves grow on woody stems.

IDEAL CONDITIONS

Temperature Normal room temperatures in summer. Rest the plant in winter at 45-50°F/7-10°C.
Light Bright, with direct sun, but not if fiercely hot.
Water Once or twice a week in summer so the compost is moist, but allow the surface to dry out between waterings. Every two or three weeks in winter to avoid the compost drying out completely.
Feed Monthly, spring to early autumn.
Pot-on Every other year in spring in a mixture of two-thirds loam-based compost and one-third sand.
Propagation Take leaf cuttings in spring.

C
Y
C
A
S

Cycas revoluta
The sago palm
originates in subtropical areas of China and Japan. In summer, the temperature is 65-80°F/18-27°C and in winter, around 55°F/13°C. Rainfall is evenly spread throughout the year. The rosette of stiff, arching fronds grows from a ball-shaped base on the compost surface that stores water against a dry period.

IDEAL CONDITIONS

Temperature A steady 65°F/18°C all year, but the palm will tolerate a winter rest at no lower than 55°F/13°C.
Water Twice a week in summer to keep compost moist; allow the surface to dry out before watering again. Every 7 to 10 days in winter in the lower temperatures.
Feed Every two weeks from late spring to early autumn.
Pot-on Every two or three years in two-thirds loam-based compost and one-third sand.
Propagation Sow seed in spring. Bottom heat of 75°F/24°C is needed.

PROBLEM

Are the leaf tips turning brown?

———— IF YES ————

CAUSE the temperature is too low.
ACTION See **IDEAL CONDITIONS**. The plant will remain in good condition only if the minimum temperature is not below 65°F/18°C.

———— IF NO ————

Is the plant in a position in the room where people brush past it?

———— IF YES ————

CAUSE Leaves are damaged by frequent touching, whether unintentionally or by fingering them.
ACTION Move the plant out of the line of traffic and resist handling the leaves.

———— IF NO ————

Are some of the frond tips touching the wall?

———— IF YES ————

CAUSE In rooms where the air is dry, the wall plaster draws moisture from any source it can – in this instance the leaves of the palm.
ACTION Move the palm so that the fronds are not actually touching the wall.

———— IF NO ————

Is the compost dry 3in/7.5cm below the surface?

———— IF YES ————

CAUSE Underwatering. Never allow the compost to dry out as much as this.
ACTION Water the compost thoroughly and then follow the watering advice in **IDEAL CONDITIONS**.

———— IF NO ————

Is the air in the room very dry?

———— IF YES ————

CAUSE Lack of humidity, although this should not be a major problem with this palm.
ACTION To be on the safe side, stand the pot on a tray of wet pebbles, or put it in a container and surround it with moist peat.

PROBLEM

Have the leaves turned yellow while the plant is flowering, and are the new buds starting to drop off?

— IF YES —

CAUSE The cyclamen has been kept too warm.
ACTION Move the plant away from radiators or fires or to a cooler room. See **IDEAL CONDITIONS**.

— IF NO —

Has the plant been in direct sunlight?

— IF YES —

CAUSE The leaves have been scorched.
ACTION Move the plant to a position where it gets bright light but no direct sunlight.

— IF NO —

Does the compost feel wet when you push in a finger, and does the top of the corm feel mushy?

— IF YES —

CAUSE The plant has been watered too often and, as a result of direct watering, the corm has started to rot.
ACTION Allow the compost to dry out and water less frequently, never directly on to the corm. The correct method is to water from below; stand the pot in shallow water so that the moisture is drawn up through the hole in the bottom of the pot. Do not leave the pot standing in water for more than 30 minutes.

— IF NO —

Are the leaves turning yellow after flowering?

— IF YES —

CAUSE This is entirely natural. All cyclamen die down for a rest period in the summer months.
ACTION None.

PROBLEM

Is the foliage scabbed; are the flower buds distorted?

— IF YES —

CAUSE Cyclamen mites, whose minute eggs on the undersides of the leaves look like dust.
ACTION If the plant is badly affected, throw it away. Otherwise, remove damaged leaves and flower buds and spray with dicofol. Repeat every few days.

Cyclamen persicum
Cyclamen come from eastern areas of the Mediterranean, where summer temperatures inland range from warm, 68°F/20°C, to hot, 82°F/28°C, and winters are cool, 45-50°F/7-10°C. Leaves are heart-shaped, light or dark green, marked with silver and white. Pink or deep red flowers, like a shuttlecock, appear from winter through to spring.

IDEAL CONDITIONS

Temperature 45-55°F/7-13°C all year.
Light Bright, but no direct sun. When the foliage dies, keep the plant in the dark.
Water Twice a week when in flower and producing leaves, once a week when no new leaves appear. Stop when leaves turn yellow and die. Store in a cool place and keep dry.
Feed Every two weeks when new growth appears. Stop at end of flowering.
Pot-on Late summer in a peat-based compost. The top of the corm should show above the surface.
Propagation Sow seed in spring or autumn.

C Y M B I D I U M

Cymbidium 'Peter Pan'
Cymbidiums are epiphytic orchids that grow on forks of trees or rocky outcrops, anchored by their roots. They are found in India and S.E. Asia where summer temperatures are 75°F/24°C, those in winter 60°F/16°C by day, slightly lower at night. The narrow leaves are bright green, flowers greenish-yellow with a crimson lip spring to early summer.

IDEAL CONDITIONS

Temperature In summer, 60-65°F/ 16-18°C, dropping at night to 50°F/10°C. In winter, 50-55°F/ 10-13°C; 45°F/7°C at night.
Light Bright, but not direct sunlight.
Water About twice a week in summer so compost is always moist but not waterlogged. Every two to three weeks in winter so compost does not dry out completely. Needs a humid atmosphere.
Feed Every two weeks, late spring to early autumn.
Pot-on In spring, every second year in orchid compost.
Propagation Divide clumps of pseudo-bulbs in spring.

PROBLEM

Are the tips of the leaves turning brown, and has the orchid failed to flower?

IF YES

CAUSE The air is too dry.
ACTION Create a humid atmosphere around the plant: see advice on page 8.

IF NO

Has the plant been kept at normal room temperatures during the winter?

IF YES

CAUSE It has been too warm. The plant must have a cooler rest period in winter.
ACTION Nothing immediately, but in late autumn move the orchid to a room with a temperature of 50-55°F/ 10-13°C. Bring it back into the warmth in spring.

IF NO

Is the plant in a shaded part of the room?

IF YES

CAUSE Not enough light.
ACTION Move the plant close to a window where it will get bright light but not direct sun. If possible, put the plant outdoors in summer in a position sheltered from direct sun and wind.

IF NO

Do the egg-shaped pseudobulbs feel soft?

IF YES

CAUSE The plant has been overwatered and the pseudobulbs are rotting.
ACTION Completely remove those pseudobulbs which have rotted. Let the compost dry out and in future water the orchid from below to avoid pouring water directly on the pseudobulbs. Place the pot in a bowl of shallow water and leave it for about 30 minutes. After removing the pot, allow excess water to drain away before returning the pot to its saucer.

OTHER SPECIES
Cymbidium devonianum is a miniature orchid, olive-green flowers, purple overmarking.

◁ PROBLEM ▷

Are the tips of the bracts turning brown?

──────────────── IF YES ────────────────

CAUSE The compost has become too dry.
ACTION Water the compost thoroughly. Thereafter stand the pot in a shallow container filled with water. Always keep the level of the water topped up, never allowing it to become dry.

──────────────── IF NO ────────────────

Is the air warm and dry?

──────────────── IF YES ────────────────

CAUSE Lack of humidity.
ACTION Create a humid atmosphere around the plant by standing the pot on a tray of wet pebbles with the base of the pot always in water. (This is entirely different advice to that given for almost all other plants – their pots should never be left in water.)

──────────────── IF NO ────────────────

Are the umbrellas turning yellow and also withering and falling?

──────────────── IF YES ────────────────

CAUSE The compost has been allowed to dry out completely.
ACTION As long as the roots themselves have not died through lack of water, the plant can be rescued. Cut off all the stems at compost level, water the compost thoroughly and leave the pot standing in shallow water. New growth will shortly appear.

──────────────── IF NO ────────────────

Does the plant look lifeless, with the bracts paling?

──────────────── IF YES ────────────────

CAUSE The plant has not been fed regularly.
ACTION Apply liquid feed to the compost every two weeks from late spring to early autumn. Do not feed during the rest of the year when the plant is resting.

OTHER SPECIES
Cyperus alternifolius 'Variegatus' has leaves and stems striped with white.

Cyperus alternifolius
The Umbrella Plant is a sedge that grows close to the water's edge in parts of Madagascar. It is one of the few plants whose roots need to be permanently damp. Temperatures are 70-80°F/21-27°C throughout the year, and most rain falls in summer; the winter is fairly dry. The tall bare stalks carry loose rosettes of green, arching bracts.

IDEAL CONDITIONS

Temperature In summer 55-65°F/ 13-18°C. Give the plant a winter rest at 50-55°F/10-13°C.
Light Bright with some direct sun, especially for variegated forms, but shade from fierce sun.
Water The compost should always be moist, so stand the pot in a saucer of water which is topped up regularly.
Feed Every two weeks, from late spring to early autumn.
Pot-on In spring in loam-based compost.
Propagation Divide when potting-on. Sow seed in spring.

D E N D R O B I U M

Dendrobium nobile
This epiphytic orchid is normally found clinging to tree branches in the humid Indian jungle, where temperatures in summer are around 75°F/24°C and in winter average 65°F/18°C. Rain falls almost daily in summer; the winter is drier. The bamboo-like pseudobulbs produce narrow, strap-shaped leaves and pink-purple blooms in early spring.

IDEAL CONDITIONS

Temperature In summer, 70-75°F/21-24°C. Rest the plant in winter at 50-55°F/10-13°C, although it will tolerate temperatures down to 45°F/7°C.
Light Bright, but not direct sun.
Water Twice a week in summer, allowing compost almost to dry out between waterings. In winter, every 7 to 10 days.
Feed Monthly, from spring to late autumn.
Pot-on Every third year in an orchid compost.
Propagation Divide when potting-on. Every section of the rhizome must have at least five pseudo-bulbs, some still to produce leaves.

◇ PROBLEM ◇

Are the leaf tips turning brown and the leaves falling?

IF YES

CAUSE The air is too dry.
ACTION Increase humidity around the plant by mist spraying each day. A longer-term effect is achieved by following the advice on page 8.

IF NO

Is the flowering period approaching?

IF YES

CAUSE Pseudobulbs about to flower shed leaves and replace them with flower stems.
ACTION Let the leaves fall of their own accord. Water more frequently, but let the compost almost dry out between waterings.

IF NO

Are there also brown marks on the leaves?

IF YES

CAUSE The orchid has been scorched by sun. It needs bright light all year round, but not direct sun.
ACTION Move it out of the sun.

PROBLEM

Has the plant failed to flower?

IF YES

CAUSE It has not had a winter rest.
ACTION Nothing can be done immediately, but see **IDEAL CONDITIONS**.

IF NO

Is the plant in a shaded part of the room?

IF YES

CAUSE Not enough light.
ACTION Move the plant closer to a window where it will get bright light but no direct sun.

OTHER SPECIES
Dendrobium aureum bears creamy yellow flowers with brown tips.

PROBLEM

Are the edges of leaves turning brown, and are whole leaves falling?

IF YES

CAUSE Lack of humidity.
ACTION Create a humid atmosphere around the plant by standing the pot on a tray of wet pebbles or by surrounding it with moist peat.

IF NO

When you push a finger into the compost does it feel dry 2-3in/5-7.5cm down?

IF YES

CAUSE The compost is much too dry.
ACTION Water thoroughly until water runs out of the drainage hole in the bottom of the pot. Then follow watering instructions in **IDEAL CONDITIONS**.

IF NO

Has the plant been near an open door or one that is often opened and closed?

IF YES

CAUSE The plant is suffering from the effect of draughts; this is most likely to happen in the winter.
ACTION Move it to a draught-free part of the room.

IF NO

Are there fine white webs on the leaves and stems?

IF YES

CAUSE Infestation by red spider mites, which are encouraged by a dry atmosphere.
ACTION Spray the plant with liquid derris and repeat every few days if the mites persist. To discourage further attacks of this pest, increase humidity, as described above.

PROBLEM

Has the plant become leggy, with bare lower stems?

IF YES

CAUSE The plant is getting old.
ACTION Rejuvenation is possible by cutting down the stems to within 5in/12.5cm of the compost. New and vigorous growth will soon appear from the cut stems.

Dieffenbachia picta
The dumb cane comes from the tropical rain forests of Brazil and Colombia. Average temperature is 75°F/24°C all year, and rainfall is plentiful. The lance-shaped leaves are green with cream or yellow markings. The sap contains calcium oxalate which is poisonous; be careful not to touch your mouth or eyes when taking cuttings.

IDEAL CONDITIONS

Temperature
65-70°F/18-21°C all year. It will tolerate a temperature down to 60°F/16°C in winter, but no lower.
Light Bright, but out of direct sun.
Water Twice a week in summer; allow the surface of the compost to dry out between waterings. Once a week in winter.
Feed Every two weeks, late spring to early autumn.
Pot-on In spring, in loam-based compost.
Propagation Take stem cuttings in early summer. Sometimes whole stems break off and, stripped of the lower leaves, these can be induced to root in water.

Dionaea muscipula
The Venus fly trap is native to bog areas of both North and South Carolina, where temperatures in summer are 65-75°F/18-24°C, in winter, 43-50°F/6-10°C. Rainfall is evenly distributed throughout the year. This plant needs constant moisture and can stand in water without harm. The stems have hinged traps with toothed edges.

IDEAL CONDITIONS

Temperature As low as possible in summer; the ideal is 50-55°F/10-13°C. Rest the plant in winter at 45-50°F/7-10°C.
Light Bright, with direct sun to give the trap good colour.
Water Twice a week during the period of active growth; the saucer must always contain water. During the winter rest, water once a week and keep the saucer dry. Use rainwater or distilled water.
Feed Monthly, spring to early autumn.
Pot-on Every two or three years in a peat/moss/sand mixture.
Propagation Divide when potting-on or sow seed in spring.

PROBLEM

Are the leaves and insect traps of the plant turning brown and dropping? Has it failed to flower?

IF YES

CAUSE The plant is not getting enough water and the air is too dry.
ACTION Stand the pot in a saucer of water, which must be regularly topped up. The plant will draw up the water it needs and the water in the saucer will provide some humidity around the plant.

IF NO

Is the plant in a shady part of the room?

IF YES

CAUSE Insufficient light. The Venus fly trap requires bright light in order to flower.
ACTION Move the plant to a sunny window. After flowers appear and fade, remove their stems completely so that the plant produces new growth instead of expending its energy on seed.

PROBLEM

Are some of the traps shut?

IF YES

CAUSE The trap has caught a fly and is digesting it.
ACTION None. When a fly, attracted by the colour of the trap and the scent of nectar, alights on the inside surface of the trap, it touches trigger hairs which cause the trap to shut. The plant then produces enzymes to digest the prey. After a few days, the trap opens again, revealing the remains. Never feed the traps with insects and certainly not with morsels of meat. Do not touch the traps out of curiosity to make them perform: this weakens the plant.

PROBLEM

Are there patches of fluffy grey mould on the plant?

IF YES

CAUSE This is *botrytis,* caused by too much watering (even for this plant) and excessive humidity.
ACTION Cut away any badly affected foliage and spray the compost with benomyl. To prevent a recurrence of the mould, increase ventilation, reduce humidity somewhat and water the plant less often.

◇ **PROBLEM** ◇

Are the leaves browning at the tips and then falling?

────── **IF YES** ──────

CAUSE The air is too dry.
ACTION Raise the humidity around the plant by putting the pot on a tray of wet pebbles or by surrounding it with moist peat. Spraying the plant daily will also help, but if the water is hard use rainwater, since lime marks the leaves.

────── **IF NO** ──────

When you push a finger into the compost does it feel dry just below the surface?

────── **IF YES** ──────

CAUSE The compost has been allowed to dry out.
ACTION Water the compost thoroughly, allowing excess water to run away. Then follow the watering advice in **IDEAL CONDITIONS**.

────── **IF NO** ──────

Has the plant been in an unheated room in winter?

────── **IF YES** ──────

CAUSE The temperature has been too low.
ACTION Move the plant to a room where the minimum temperature is 60°F/16°C..

────── **IF NO** ──────

Are there hard brown lumps on stems and under leaves?

────── **IF YES** ──────

CAUSE An attack by scale insects.
ACTION If only a few, scrape them off with fingernail; if many, spray with malathion.

────── **PROBLEM** ──────

Is the plant leggy, with bare lower stems?

────── **IF YES** ──────

CAUSE This is natural as the plant grows old.
ACTION Drastic, but effective: cut back the stem to about 6in/15cm, making the cut just above a node (the point at which there was a leaf until it fell off). In time, new growth will emerge from the cut stem.

Dizygotheca elegantissima
False aralia comes from tropical rain forest areas of Vanuatu in the western Pacific. Humidity here is always high, with wet summers and slightly drier winters; temperatures are 75-80°F/24-27°C all year. The leaves are divided into fine, glossy leaflets with serrated edges. Their coppery colour changes to dark green as they mature.

IDEAL CONDITIONS

Temperature As far as is possible a constant 65°F/18°C in summer. Rest plants in winter at 60°F/16°C, but no lower.
Light Bright, but shade from direct sun.
Water Twice a week in summer so that the compost is always moist. Once a week is sufficient in winter, but do not allow the compost to dry out. Needs humidity.
Feed Every two weeks, from late spring to early autumn.
Pot-on Every second year in spring in peat-based compost.
Propagation Sow seed in spring.

Dracaena marginata
'Tricolor'
Dracaena is a native of
the tropical rain forest of
Madagascar, off the east
coast of Africa. It is hot,
70-80°F/21-27°C, all
year, humidity is high
and rain plentiful. The
plant forms a rosette of
narrow, pointed arching
leaves, striped green,
cream and pink. When
mature, it has a thin
woody stem.

IDEAL CONDITIONS

Temperature
65-75°F/18-24°C all
year, although it will
tolerate a drop to
60°F/16°C in winter,
and no lower.
Light Bright, but
protect it from direct
sunlight.
Water In summer,
twice a week so that
the compost is always
moist. Every 7 to 10
days should be
enough in winter. The
compost should
never be allowed to
dry out completely.
Feed Every two
weeks from late
spring to early
autumn.
Pot-on In spring in
loam-based compost.
Propagation Take
stem cuttings in
summer.

PROBLEM

Are the leaves looking pale and washed out?

IF YES

CAUSE Not enough light. If the dracaena is to keep the
brilliant colour which is a major part of its attraction, it
must have bright light.
ACTION Move it nearer to a well-lit window, but out of
direct sunlight.

PROBLEM

Are leaf edges turning brown and whole leaves
yellowing and falling?

IF YES

CAUSE The air is too dry.
ACTION Increase humidity around the plant by standing the pot on a tray of wet pebbles or surrounding it
with moist peat. Mist spray the leaves regularly.

IF NO

When you push a finger into the compost does it feel
dry just below the surface?

IF YES

CAUSE Underwatering.
ACTION Water the plant thoroughly; then follow the
watering routine in **IDEAL CONDITIONS**.

IF NO

Has the plant been kept in a cold room in winter?

IF YES

CAUSE The temperature has been too low.
ACTION Remove badly affected leaves. Move the
plant to a warmer room, where the temperature is
65-75°F/18-24°C and never below 60°F/16°C for any
length of time.

IF NO

Have you had the plant for two or more years?

IF YES

CAUSE As a plant matures, it naturally sheds its lower
leaves and develops a woody stem.
ACTION There is nothing that can be done to halt this
natural process.

PROBLEM

Are there brown marks on the leaves?

IF YES

CAUSE The plant has been underwatered.
ACTION Water the compost until any excess runs out through the drainage hole of the pot. Thereafter water as in **IDEAL CONDITIONS**. The compost should never be allowed to dry out completely.

IF NO

Has water fallen on the leaves during watering?

IF YES

CAUSE The leaves will scorch if the plant is exposed to strong sunlight when the leaves are wet.
ACTION In future, water the plant from below. Place the pot in a bowl in 2-3in/5-7.5cm of water. Leave it for about 30 minutes until drops of moisture are seen on the surface of the compost. Let excess water drain away before putting it back on its saucer.

IF NO

Do the leaves feel soft and mushy near the base?

IF YES

CAUSE Excessive watering, which makes the plant liable to stem rot disease.
ACTION If all leaves are affected, crown rot has set in, and you will have to throw the plant away. If only a few leaves are rotting, remove them completely. Dust the compost with a fungicide powder; let it dry out and then follow the watering routine in **IDEAL CONDITIONS**.

PROBLEM

Are all the leaves shrivelling.

IF YES

CAUSE This is due to underwatering.
ACTION Water thoroughly. The lower leaves tend to shrivel in winter; once they are completely dead, pull them away cleanly.

OTHER SPECIES

Echeveria harmsii has a rosette of lance-shaped leaves covered with soft hairs.

Echeveria derenbergii
This succulent is from high, unforested areas of Mexico. In summer, temperatures are 60-75°F/16-24°C; in winter, somewhat lower. Rain falls throughout the year, but mostly in summer. The rosettes of fleshy, grey-green leaves, tipped with red, contain reserves of water, drawn on in dry spells; early summer flowers are orange-red.

IDEAL CONDITIONS

Temperature In summer, normal room temperatures. In winter, rest the plants at 50-55°F/10-13°C. They will tolerate temperatures down to 45°F/7°C, but any frost will damage them.
Light Bright, with direct sun, but shade from fierce sunlight.
Water Once or twice a week in summer; in winter, once in two or three weeks.
Feed Monthly, from spring to early autumn.
Pot-on In spring, in loam-based compost with sand added.
Propagation Take stem cuttings in summer, or remove offsets when potting-on the main plant.

Echinocereus pectinatus
The hedgehog cactus is
found in desert areas of
Mexico. Temperatures
by day can reach
100°F/38°C, dropping
fast at night to give
ground frost. Rainfall is
erratic. The fleshy stem,
with 25 ribs, holds a
reserve of water which
is used in dry spells.
The ribs are covered
with pink spines, turning
white; pink bell flowers
bloom in summer.

IDEAL CONDITIONS

Temperature Normal
room temperatures in
summer; it can stand
up to 80°F/27°C. In
winter it should rest
at about 45°F/7°C.
Light Very bright
with plenty of direct
sun all year round.
Water Once or twice
a week in summer. In
winter do not water if
the cactus is kept
cool. In warm rooms,
water about once a
month so the compost
does not dry out
altogether.
Feed Monthly, spring
to early autumn.
Pot-on In spring in a
mixture of loam-
based compost and
sand or grit.
Propagation Stem
cuttings in summer,
or seed in spring.

PROBLEM

Has the cactus failed to flower? Are the spines
dull in colour?

IF YES

CAUSE Not enough light. It will flower only if it has good
light with full sun throughout the year.
ACTION Move the cactus to a sunnier spot. Good light is
especially important during winter in the build-up to
the next summer's flowering. Poor light also makes
the spines dull and lifeless. However, the pink spines
on a young plant do turn white as it matures.

IF NO

Has the plant been in a warm room in winter?

IF YES

CAUSE The plant has been denied a winter rest.
ACTION Nothing now, but in late autumn move the plant
to a room with a temperature around 45°F/7°C. Bring
into the warmth in early spring.

PROBLEM

Does the stem look bloated?

IF YES

CAUSE Overwatering. The stem is a water reservoir,
but when it reaches the limit of its capacity it swells.
ACTION Allow the compost to dry out and then follow
the routine of watering in **IDEAL CONDITIONS**.

IF NO

Does the base of the stem also feel soft and mushy?

IF YES

CAUSE Even greater overwatering. In summer a combination of waterlogged compost and poor ventilation
is a double encouragement to rot. To cut down the
risk, keep the compost just moist in summer and place
the plant near an open window or outdoors if possible.
ACTION If the whole stem is affected, there is nothing
that can be done; get rid of the plant.

OTHER SPECIES
Echinocereus knippelianus forms clumps of
fine, ribbed stems with short spines and bears
pale pink flowers in spring and summer.

PROBLEM

Has the plant refused to flower?

IF YES

CAUSE It has not had a winter rest period.
ACTION Nothing at the moment, but in late autumn move the plant to a room with a temperature in the range 50-55°F/10-13°C to encourage it to flower the following year.

IF NO

Has the plant been in a shaded part of the room?

IF YES

CAUSE Not enough light.
ACTION Move the plant closer to a window where it will get bright light, but not direct sun. Good light is particularly important in the short daylight hours of winter.

PROBLEM

Have the flower buds fallen before opening?

IF YES

CAUSE Underwatering. Once flower buds start to form keep the compost moist, but not waterlogged.
ACTION Water the compost thoroughly until water begins to appear through the drainage hole in the pot. Thereafter water as in IDEAL CONDITIONS.

IF NO

Has the plant been near an open door or one that is opened and closed frequently?

IF YES

CAUSE Draughts, to which epiphyllums are sensitive.
ACTION Move the plant to a draught-free part of the room. Unfortunately moving a plant which is in bud may in itself cause buds to fall, so it is better to make sure that there are no draughts in the first place.

PROBLEM

Do the stems look soft and shrivelled?

IF YES

CAUSE Underwatering, especially in winter.
ACTION Water the compost and ensure that it never dries out altogether.

Epiphyllum 'Ackermanii'
The orchid cactus is a jungle plant from Central America, where it grows as an epiphyte on trees. The climate is warm – 75°F/24°C – with rain all year. The flattened stems, covered with bristles, grow long and may need support, especially when the large heads of red, cup-shaped flowers appear in late spring.

IDEAL CONDITIONS

Temperature In summer, 65-75°F/18-24°C. Rest the plant in winter at 50-55°F/10-13°C.
Light Bright, but not direct sun. Put plants outdoors in the shade in summer.
Water Once or twice a week in summer. Every two weeks in winter; the compost should not dry out completely.
Feed Once a month from the appearance of flower buds until early autumn.
Pot-on In spring in loam-based compost with added sand.
Propagation Take cuttings in summer, 5in/12.5cm long, allowing them to dry for a day or two before potting-up.

EUONYMUS

Euonymus japonicus
'Aureo-variegatus'
This Euonymus is an evergreen shrub from the temperate forests of Japan, where summers are 70°F/21°C and winters 45°F/7°C, but summer can be hotter and winter much cooler. Rain falls throughout the year, with heavy monsoon downpours in late summer. The dark green, laurel-shaped leaves are marked with yellow.

IDEAL CONDITIONS

Temperature In summer around 55°F/13°C, but it can stand temperatures up to 65°F/18°C. It must have a cool rest period at 45°F/7°C to keep its good looks.
Light Bright, but shade from direct sun in summer. In winter weak sunlight will help to maintain good leaf colour.
Water Twice a week in summer but let the surface of the compost dry out between waterings. In winter, once a week.
Feed Every two weeks, late spring to early autumn.
Pot-on In spring in loam-based compost.
Propagation Take stem cuttings in summer.

PROBLEM

Have the lower leaves started to fall?

IF YES

CAUSE If this happens in winter, it is usually because the plant is not kept sufficiently cool.
ACTION Move the plant to a room where the temperature is around 45°F/7°C In winter the plant will suffer in temperatures above 50-55°F/10-13°C.

IF NO

Are there fine white threads on leaves and stems?

IF YES

CAUSE The plant has been attacked by red spider mites, encouraged by dry, warm conditions.
ACTION Spray with liquid derris, repeating the treatment every few days until all the pests disappear. If the plant cannot be kept at a low temperature, increase humidity around the plant: see page 8.

IF NO

Are there hard brown bumps on the underside of leaves?

IF YES

CAUSE These are sap-sucking scale insects. If there are only a few, scrape them off with a fingernail; if the infestation is heavy, spray with malathion.

IF NO

Is there a white powdery deposit on the leaves?

IF YES

CAUSE This is mildew, encouraged by poor ventilation.
ACTION Remove any badly affected leaves, and spray the plant with benomyl.

PROBLEM

Is the plant's growth getting out of hand?

IF YES

CAUSE Typical, but it can be kept in check.
ACTION Prune stems in spring and regularly pinch out growing tips to promote bushiness. Cut away any stems with completely green leaves or the whole plant may revert to plain green foliage.

◁ **PROBLEM** ▷

Are the leaves brown at the edges? Are they turning yellow and falling? Are the flowers and bracts dropping?

═══════════════ **IF YES** ═══════════════

CAUSE The air is evidently too dry.
ACTION Increase humidity around the plant by standing the pot on a tray of wet pebbles or by surrounding it with moist peat. Daily mist spraying helps.

═══════════════ **IF NO** ═══════════════

Has the plant been in an unheated room?

═══════════════ **IF YES** ═══════════════

CAUSE The temperature has been too low.
ACTION Move the plant to a warmer room where the temperature is a steady 65°F/18°C.. The lowest temperature the plant can tolerate is 55°F/13°C.

═══════════════ **IF NO** ═══════════════

Has the plant been in a shaded part of the room?

═══════════════ **IF YES** ═══════════════

CAUSE Not enough light.
ACTION Move it closer to a window, but not into direct sunlight.

═══════════════ **IF NO** ═══════════════

Are the bracts starting to fade and fall in late winter and early spring?

═══════════════ **IF YES** ═══════════════

CAUSE This is entirely natural. The plant is usually sold just before Christmas when colourful plants are scarce; and while the bracts remain brilliant for many weeks, they will eventually fade and drop. At this stage, the plant is often thrown away, but if the advice below is followed there is a good chance that it can be induced to produce new bracts later in the year.
ACTION Prune all stems to within 6in/15cm of the surface of the compost. Water about once a week so that the compost does not dry out completely, and water often when new growth appears. In late autumn put the plant into a room at a steady 65°F/18°C. For the next eight weeks it must have 10 hours of daylight and 14 hours of total darkness; this is essential for success. Then move the plant into normal light, and new bracts should begin to appear.

Euphorbia pulcherrima
The poinsettia
originates in forested mountain areas of Mexico. Normal temperature is around 70°F/21°C, but is often much hotter. Humidity and rainfall are high thoughout the year. Leaves are oval, toothed and mid-green; red, pink or white bracts, surrounding white flowers, are produced in winter.

IDEAL CONDITIONS

Temperature A steady 65°F/18°C all year; never below 55°F/13°C.
Light Bright, but no direct sun in summer. For about eight weeks in mid-autumn it must have 10 hours of daylight and 14 hours of complete darkness if it is to produce bracts.
Water Twice a week in summer when new growth is established. Once a week for rest of the year.
Feed Every two weeks after new growth starts until early autumn.
Pot-on In late spring in loam-or peat-based compost.
Propogation Stem cuttings in early summer.

× Fatshedera lizei
The ivy tree is a hybrid developed from *Fatsia japonica*, a native of Japan, and *Hedera helix* 'Hibernica' the Irish ivy. Both plants are accustomed to temperate climates, with summers around 60°F/16°C, and winters of 45-50°/7-10°C. Rainfall is evenly spread throughout the year. The dark green, glossy leaves are ivy-shaped.

IDEAL CONDITIONS

Temperature In summer, around 55°F/13°C, but it will tolerate temperatures up to 65°F/18°C. Give the plant a rest at 45-50°F/7-10°C in winter
Light Bright, but no direct sun. It will grow in a slightly shady position, but variegated forms must have bright light and no shade.
Water Twice a week in summer to keep compost always moist. In winter every 10 to 14 days.
Feed Every two weeks, late spring to early autumn.
Pot-on In spring in loam-based compost.
Propagation Stem cuttings in early summer.

◇ PROBLEM ◇

Are the leaves growing distorted? Are there yellow patches on them, and are some of them falling?

IF YES

CAUSE The plant has been attacked by aphids. This usually occurs in late spring and early summer.
ACTION Spray with pyrethrum. Repeat until all the aphids are destroyed.

IF NO

Are there fine white webs on leaves and stems?

IF YES

CAUSE An attack by red spider mites, normally encouraged by a dry atmosphere.
ACTION Remove badly affected leaves and spray with liquid derris every few days until the pests disappear. To discourage them in future, mist spray the plant daily. If temperatures are at the higher end of the range, increase humidity: see page 8.

IF NO

Are the leaves falling, even if there is no apparent damage and no sign of insects?

IF YES

CAUSE The plant has not had enough water.
ACTION Water the compost thoroughly and never let it dry out completely.

PROBLEM

If it is a variegated fatshedera, are the leaves paling and losing their rich colour?

IF YES

CAUSE Poor light.
ACTION Move the plant close to a window where it will get good light, but no direct sun.

PROBLEM

Is the plant becoming leggy, with bare lower stems?

IF YES

CAUSE Entirely natural.
ACTION In spring, cut back leggy stems to within 4in/10cm of the compost. Pinch out growing tips to encourage bushy growth.

PROBLEM

Are the leaves shrivelling, with the edges turning brown, then turning yellow and dropping off?

IF YES

CAUSE When this happens in winter it is usually because the room is too warm for the plant.
ACTION Move it to a room where the temperature is below 45°F/7°C. Remove badly affected leaves.

IF NO

If it is happening in summer, is the air dry?

IF YES

CAUSE Lack of humidity and warm weather.
ACTION Make the heat more tolerable by increasing humidity: see page 8.

IF NO

When you push a finger into the compost is it dry 2-3in/5-7.5cm below the surface?

IF YES

CAUSE The compost is much too dry.
ACTION Water thoroughly, allowing any excess to drain away before returning the pot to its saucer. Then follow the watering instructions in **IDEAL CONDITIONS**.

IF NO

Is the plant in a sunny part of the room?

IF YES

CAUSE The leaves have been scorched.
ACTION Move the plant out of the direct line of the sun.

IF NO

CAUSE The plant may merely be shedding some of its lower leaves, which is natural.
ACTION Nothing can be done to prevent this.

PROBLEM

Is the plant growing inconveniently big?

IF YES

CAUSE A fatsia quickly grows to about 5ft/1.5m, but it can be checked.
ACTION Prune the stems by about half in spring. The plant will then grow bushier.

Fatsia japonica
Fatsia japonica is an evergreen shrub from temperate and sub-tropical forest areas of Japan. In temperate areas, summers are around 60°F/16°C, rising to 80°F/27°C in the sub-tropics. Winter temperatures are 45-50°F/7-10°C, but can be much lower. The large, glossy, mid-green leaves are deeply dissected.

IDEAL CONDITIONS

Temperature In summer 55-60°F/13-16°C; in higher temperatures growth is soft and poor. Rest the plant in winter at about 45°F/7°C.
Light Bright, but no direct sun. In winter good light is very important.
Water Twice a week in summer to keep compost moist but not waterlogged. Every 7 to 10 days in winter in a cool room. Allow the surface to dry out before watering again.
Feed Every two weeks, late spring to early autumn.
Pot-on In spring in loam-based compost.
Propagation Take stem cuttings in early summer.

F E R O C A C T U S

Ferocactus latispinus
This is a cactus from the desert areas of Mexico. Daytime temperatures may be up to 100°F/38°C, falling rapidly to give ground frost at night. Rainfall is erratic, usually in short bursts. The globular ball, with red and white spines, has a reserve of water against drought. Mature plants may bear red flowers in summer.

IDEAL CONDITIONS

Temperature In summer, normal room temperatures. In winter, rest it at 48°F/9°C.
Light Bright, with direct sun all year.
Water Twice a week in summer, but let the surface of the compost dry out between waterings. In winter every two to three weeks. Plants in a low temperature need less frequent watering, but the compost should not dry out completely.
Feed Every two weeks, late spring to early autumn.
Pot-on In spring in one part sharp sand to three parts peat-based compost.
Propagation Sow seed in spring.

PROBLEM

Are the spines losing their colour? Have the flower buds either not opened or not appeared at all?

IF YES

CAUSE Not enough light.
ACTION Move the plant to a position where it will get direct sun all year round. Only bright sun will maintain good colour in the spines and encourage flowering. However, the cactus will not flower until it is mature, roughly when about 4in/10cm across.

IF NO

Has the cactus been kept in a centrally heated room during the winter?

IF YES

CAUSE It has not had the winter rest period it needs. This has inhibited flowering and led to poor growth.
ACTION Nothing immediately, but in the late autumn move the plant to a room with a temperature around 48°F/9°C where it will get direct sun.

PROBLEM

Are there fine white webs between the spines?

IF YES

CAUSE Infestation by red spider mites, which like the dry conditions in which the cactus flourishes.
ACTION Spray with liquid derris and repeat if the insects persist. This plant does not need increased humidity, but, at least in summer, make sure that the compost does not dry out. Mites may attack in winter if the cactus is kept in a warm, dry, room.

PROBLEM

Are there brown to yellow patches on the stem? Does the stem feel soft at the base?

IF YES

CAUSE Stem rot, encouraged by too-frequent watering.
ACTION If the whole cactus is affected, throw it away. Otherwise dust the compost with fungicide powder and let it dry out. Remove the plant from the pot, wash the compost away from the roots and remove any which are soft and rotted. Repot in fresh compost, which has been soaked in fungicide. Thereafter water as in **IDEAL CONDITIONS**.

PROBLEM

Are the leaves turning yellow and dropping? Is growth generally poor?

Ficus benjamina
The weeping fig is native to tropical rain forests of S.E. Asia. Climate is hot (75-80°F/24-27°C) and humid – rain falls all year round. Stems are woody, and the pointed leaves are light green, darkening with age. Foliage is naturally drooping and is not necessarily a sign that anything is amiss with the plant.

IF YES

CAUSE Poor light.
ACTION Move the plant closer to a window, where it will get good light, but it must be out of direct sunlight which can scorch the leaves.

IF NO

When you push a finger into the compost does it feel wet just below the surface?

IF YES

CAUSE Overwatering. The compost has become waterlogged, starving the roots of oxygen.
ACTION Allow the compost to dry out and then follow the watering instructions in **IDEAL CONDITIONS**.

IF NO

Are there soft, light brown and hard, dark brown bumps on the underside of leaves?

IF YES

CAUSE The bumps are scale insects, which suck the sap and cause yellow blemishes on the leaves.
ACTION If there are only a few, scrape them off with a fingernail. Otherwise, spray the plant with malathion, spraying again a few days later if the insects persist.

IF NO

Are there fine white webs on the leaves and stems?

IF YES

CAUSE Red spider mites, which also suck the sap.
ACTION Spray with liquid derris and repeat the treatment if necessary. Increase humidity around the plant by mist spraying daily, using rainwater if tap water is hard.

IF NO

Are the leaves falling in winter?

IF YES

CAUSE This is entirely natural. The plant will shed older leaves, but they will be replaced by new growth in spring.

IDEAL CONDITIONS

Temperature All year at 65-75°F/18-24°C, but the plant fares better if it has a short winter rest at around 60°F/16°C. High temperatures, with limited winter light, encourage weak growth.
Light Bright, but out of direct sun at all times.
Water Twice a week in summer, once a week in winter – more often if in a warm room.
Feed Every two weeks, late spring to early autumn.
Pot-on Every second year in spring in a mixture of loam, peat, leaf-mould and sand.
Propagation Take stem cuttings in summer.

FITTONIA

Fittonia verschaffeltii
Fittonia is a creeping plant from tropical rain forests of Peru, where it carpets the ground, lower trunks of trees and rocks. Climate is hot (80°F/27°C) and humid, with rainfall high all year. Indoors, warmth and humidity are vital if the plants are not to grow straggly. The dark green, oval leaves have carmine veins.

IDEAL CONDITIONS

Temperature In summer, 65-70°F/18-21°C. In winter the plant does better if given a short rest at 60°F/16°C, but no lower. It needs a humid atmosphere.
Light It wants a slightly shaded spot, except in winter when it must have a brighter light.
Water Twice a week in summer so that the compost is always moist. Once a week in winter.
Feed Every two weeks, late spring to early autumn.
Pot-on In spring in a mix of two parts peat-based compost to one part sharp sand.
Propagation Take stem cuttings in early summer.

◁ PROBLEM ▷

Do the leaves look papery and dull? Are they shrivelling and curling at the edges?

IF YES

CAUSE The air in the room is too dry for this plant.
ACTION Increase the humidity around it by standing the pot on a tray of wet pebbles or surrounding it with moist peat. Spray the plant daily with tepid water, using rainwater if the mains water is hard; since lime marks the leaves.

IF NO

When you push a finger into the compost does it feel dry well below the surface?

IF YES

CAUSE Underwatering. For this plant, the compost should always be moist in summer.
ACTION Water thoroughly, then follow the watering instructions in **IDEAL CONDITIONS**.

IF NO

Is the plant near a sunny window?

IF YES

CAUSE The leaves have been scorched. Fittonias do not like direct sun.
ACTION Move the plant to a slightly shady spot – not a gloomy corner, or the leaf colour will be poor.

IF NO

Are the leaves also falling?

IF YES

CAUSE The room is too cold and draughty; this is most likely to be the case in winter.
ACTION Put the plant in a draught-free spot in a room where the temperature is no lower than 60°F/16°C.

PROBLEM

Have the stems become bare and straggly?

IF YES

CAUSE This is the way the plant grows naturally.
ACTION In winter, cut back stems to about 3in/7.5cm and, as new stems grow, pinch out the tips to encourage bushiness.

PROBLEM

Are the leaves wilting and falling, and are buds and flowers dropping?

━━━━━━━━━ IF YES ━━━━━━━━━

CAUSE Not enough water. If the compost has dried out the whole plant will appear in a state of collapse.
ACTION Water thoroughly until the excess runs out through the drainage hole of the pot. In a short time, if the wilting has been spotted soon enough, the plant will perk up.

━━━━━━━━━ IF NO ━━━━━━━━━

Has the plant been near a sunny window?

━━━━━━━━━ IF YES ━━━━━━━━━

CAUSE Too much direct sun. Buds and flowers will fall rapidly if the plant gets too hot.
ACTION Move the plant out of the sun, preferably to a well-ventilated spot near an open window. A spell outdoors in the shade is beneficial. Remove faded flowers and seed pods (green, turning purple) to encourage the plant to produce more flowers.

━━━━━━━━━ IF NO ━━━━━━━━━

Are there green or black insects on foliage and buds?

━━━━━━━━━ IF YES ━━━━━━━━━

CAUSE The plant is infested with aphids.
ACTION Spray with pyrethrum, repeating every few days while the insects persist. Dry air encourages aphids, so mist spray the plants daily to deter them.

━━━━━━━━━ IF NO ━━━━━━━━━

Are there fine white webs on leaves and stems?

━━━━━━━━━ IF YES ━━━━━━━━━

CAUSE Red spider mites, which also like dry air.
ACTIONS Spray the plants with liquid derris and increase humidity by regular mist spraying.

━━━━━━━━━ IF NO ━━━━━━━━━

Are the leaves falling when flowering is over?

━━━━━━━━━ IF YES ━━━━━━━━━

CAUSE This is entirely natural.
ACTION Cut back all stems to 6in/15cm long and rest the plant at 50-55°F/10-13°C, watering occasionally.

Fuchsia magellanica **Most hybrid fuchsias** have been developed from this plant, which is native to mountain areas of Mexico, Peru and Chile. Average temperature is 60°F/16°C, and rain falls throughout the year. Fuchsias are grown as bushy shrubs or to trail. The white, red or pink bell-shaped flowers appear from late spring to early autumn.

IDEAL CONDITIONS

Temperature When new growth starts, keeps the plant in the range 55-65°F/13-18°C – the lower end is better. Rest it in winter at 50-55°F/10-13°C
Light Bright, but shade from hot sun.
Water Two or three times a week in summer to keep compost always moist. In winter, water about once a month to prevent the compost from drying out completely.
Feed Every week, late spring to early autumn.
Pot-on In early spring in loam- or peat-based compost.
Propagation Take stem cuttings in spring and summer.

Guzmania lingulata
Guzmanias are epiphytic bromeliads from Central and South American tropical rain forests. The climate is hot (80°F/27°C) and humid, with plenty of rain all year. The plants grow in forks of trees and on rocks. Sword-shaped green leaves, tinged red, are crowned by crimson bracts and yellow flowers, autumn to winter.

IDEAL CONDITIONS

Temperature In summer, 65-70°F/18-21°C. In winter 60-65°F/16-18°C. Needs a humid atmosphere all year round.
Light Bright if it is to flower successfully, but shade from fierce sunlight.
Water Twice a week in summer; pour some into the centre of the rosette. Once a week in winter, but not into the rosette. Use rainwater if mains water is hard.
Feed Once a month, from spring to early autumn.
Pot-on Unnecessary; the main plant dies, leaving offsets.
Propagation Remove the offsets when they are well established.

PROBLEM

Are the tips of leaves or whole leaves turning brown and becoming dry?

IF YES

CAUSE The air in the room has been too dry.
ACTION Increase humidity: see page 8. Mist spraying from above each day will also help. If mains water is hard, use rainwater to avoid unsightly lime deposits on the leaves.

IF NO

When you push a finger into the compost does it feel dry about 2in/5cm down?

IF YES

CAUSE The compost has been allowed to dry out.
ACTION Water the compost until water runs out of the drainage hole in the pot. Thereafter, follow watering advice in **IDEAL CONDITIONS**..

PROBLEM

Are the bright red bracts beginning to fade, and is the whole plant starting to die back?

IF YES

CAUSE This is the natural cycle of the plant.
ACTION Before dying, the main plant will produce offsets, which can be removed when they are well developed – at least 3in/7.5cm long. Plant them in a peat-based compost.

PROBLEM

Have the leaves turned brown and mushy at the base of the plant?

IF YES

CAUSE Overwatering and excessive humidity.
ACTION None, since the plant is rotting. It may recover when the compost has dried out, but this is unlikely. If only a few leaves have been affected, remove them and dust the compost with a fungicide powder.

OTHER SPECIES

Guzmania zahnii has long, translucent leaves, striped red both on top and underneath. Deep red bracts surround white flowers.

PROBLEM

Are the leaves turning a reddish colour and shrivelling?

IF YES

CAUSE The plant has been in direct sun.
ACTION Move it to a part of the room where it will be out of the sun or, if that is not possible, to a room with a sunless window but good light.

IF NO

When you push a finger into the compost does it feel dry about 2in/5cm down?

IF YES

CAUSE Underwatering. Leaves are likely to shrivel if the compost has dried out for any length of time. The fleshy leaves store water, but when that has been used up they start to shrivel. This is most likely to happen in the winter, when the plant needs less frequent watering and so may be neglected.
ACTION Water the compost thoroughly until excess water runs through the drainage hole in the pot. Then follow the watering instructions in **IDEAL CONDITIONS**. If the plant is in a shallow pot, the compost will dry out more rapidly, so keep close watch on it.

PROBLEM

Are the leaves changing from dark to light green?

IF YES

CAUSE The plant has not had enough light, possibly because it has been in too shady a part of the room.
ACTION Move it closer to the window so that it gets bright light, but no direct sun. In time the colour will deepen with good light.

PROBLEM

Do the leaves look and feel soft?

IF YES

CAUSE Overwatering. The tissue in the leaves can store only so much water. If the compost is kept sodden, bloating and rotting are likely.
ACTION Let the compost dry out, then follow the watering routine in **IDEAL CONDITIONS**. Too much water will also make the plant rot at its base; if the plant has reached this state it is best discarded.

Haworthia margaritifera
Haworthia is a succulent native to Cape Province, South Africa. It grows among rocks and short grass in dry, hot areas – 65-80°F/18-27°C in summer, in winter 45-50°F/7-10°C. Winters are wet, summers fairly dry. Dark green, fleshy leaves with pearly warts form a rosette. Small white flowers in summer and early autumn.

IDEAL CONDITIONS

Temperature Normal room temperatures in summer; even a period of very hot weather will not harm the plant. Winter rest at 45°F/7°C.
Light Bright, but shade from direct sun.
Water Twice a week in summer, so compost is always moist. In winter, once a month if in a low temperature, but compost must not dry out completely.
Feed Monthly, from spring to early autumn.
Pot-on In spring in two parts loam-based compost to one part sand in a shallow pot.
Propagation Remove offsets when potting-on the main plant.

Hedera helix
So-called English ivy is found throughout Europe, where summers are dry and warm, 60-70°F/16-21°C, and winters wet and cool, 45-50°F/7-10°C. Three- to five-lobed dark green leaves are borne on stems which, outdoors, will trail along the ground, climb up trees or creep along walls.

IDEAL CONDITIONS

Temperature Ivies do not like hot summers and thrive best below 65°F/18°C, with a winter rest at 50°F/10°C.
Light Bright, no direct sun. They will grow in slightly shaded spots.
Water Once or twice a week in summer, to keep compost always moist. In winter, every 7 to 10 days; plants in a cool room need less watering.
Feed Every two weeks, late spring to early autumn.
Pot-on In spring, in a mixture of loam, peat, sand and leaf-mould or in loam-based compost plus sand.
Propagation Take stem cuttings in summer.

PROBLEM

Are the edges of the leaves turning brown and papery? Is growth generally spindly?

IF YES

CAUSE The room has been too warm and the light too poor. This combination is most likely in the winter.
ACTION Move the plant to a cooler room with a temperature no higher than 50°F/10°C. Put it close to a window so that it gets the best of the restricted winter daylight. In summer, try to keep the plant in a temperature below 65°F/18°C. Any bare stems should be cut back in spring to within a few inches of the compost. When new growth is established, pinch out growing tips to encourage bushiness.

IF NO

Are there fine white webs on leaves and stems?

IF YES

CAUSE An invasion of red spider mites.
ACTION Spray the plant with liquid derris and respray every few days while the insects persist. Discourage them in future by regular mist spraying. Periodic washing of the tough leaves under running water will dislodge insects and keep the leaves dust-free.

IF NO

Are there green and black insects on the foliage?

IF YES

CAUSE These are aphids, which suck the sap.
ACTION Spray with liquid derris, repeating if necessary.

PROBLEM

Are variegated leaves reverting to plain green?

IF YES

CAUSE Not enough light.
ACTION Move the ivy closer to a window, but out of direct sun. Cut stems with green leaves back to the first variegated leaf.

OTHER SPECIES
Hedera canariensis 'Variegata' has large, green leaves with broad, creamy-white edges.

PROBLEM

Are the leaves curling and dropping? Are buds falling before they open properly?

IF YES

CAUSE The air is too dry.
ACTION Mist spray the plant daily in spring and summer. For a longer-term increase in humidity, stand the pot on a tray of wet pebbles or surround it with moist peat.

IF NO

Has the plant been in a cool or unheated room?

IF YES

CAUSE The plant has not been warm enough.
ACTION Move the plant to a room at a steady 60-65°F/16-18°C. Hibiscus should at no time be kept in a temperature below 55°F/13°C.

IF NO

When you push a finger into the compost does it feel dry about 2in/5cm down?

IF YES

CAUSE The compost has been allowed to dry out. Buds and leaves drop at a dramatic rate when this is allowed to happen.
ACTION Water the compost thoroughly. Then follow watering instructions in **IDEAL CONDITIONS**.

PROBLEM

Has the hibiscus failed to flower?

IF YES

CAUSE Not enough light.
ACTION Move the plant to a sunny window, but shade from scorching sun.

PROBLEM

Are there green and black insects clinging to flower buds and leaves?

IF YES

CAUSE These are aphids, which suck sap from the leaves and distort the growth of flower buds.
ACTION Spray the plant with pyrethrum and repeat if the aphids persist.

Hibiscus rosa-sinensis
This hibiscus is an evergreen shrub, found in subtropical forests of S.E. Asia, with a temperature of around 75°F/24°C all year. The climate is humid, with most rain in spring and summer. The dark green, glossy leaves have serrated edges, single or double funnel-shaped flowers – red, pink, orange or yellow – bloom all summer.

IDEAL CONDITIONS

Temperature In summer 60-65°F/16-18°C. Rest the plant in winter at 55-60°F/13-16°C, but no lower. Needs humidity in warm weather.
Light Bright, with direct sun to encourage flowering. Shade only from scorching sun.
Water Twice a week in summer, so compost is always moist. Once a week in winter should be enough.
Feed Every two weeks from late spring to early autumn.
Pot-on In spring in loam-based compost.
Propagation Take stem cuttings in summer.

Hippeastrum hybrids
Hippeastrums, often
wrongly called
amaryllis, are native to
Brazil and Mexico,
where summers are hot
and winters warm
(55°F/13°C). Rain falls
all year, most in
summer. The bulb
needs a dormant period
to flower. Leaves are
strap-shaped, flowers
like trumpets – white,
red, pink, orange or
streaked – midwinter to
early spring.

IDEAL CONDITIONS

Temperature In
summer 55-60°F/13-
16°C. When foliage
has died down in
mid- to late autumn,
store the bulb at
50°F/10°C. Start into
growth in late winter
in a warm room,
65-70°F/18-21°C.
Light Bright, direct
sun when in growth.
Water Two or three
times a week in
summer. When
foliage yellows, stop
watering. Store bulb
dry. Start watering
again in late winter.
Feed Every two
weeks, late spring
until foliage dies.
Pot-on Every third
year in late winter in
loam-based compost.
Propagation Remove
offsets when potting-
on.

PROBLEM

Has the bulb produced leaves in its second year
but failed to flower?

IF YES

CAUSE The conditions in which the bulb has been kept
after its previous flowering have not allowed it to build
up its strength for flowering again.
ACTION In the summer months, put the pot in a sunny
window where it will get a good baking. Better still,
put it outdoors where it will get sun all day long. In this
way, the bulb builds itself up to flower the following
year. It must also be fed regularly during this period,
as in **IDEAL CONDITIONS**. Without the correct treatment,
it is likely to become smaller each year and the
chance of its flowering again will be remote.

PROBLEM

Has the flower stem not apeared until late spring?

IF YES

CAUSE It has not been kept warm enough.
ACTION The bulb needs a temperature of 65-70°/18-
21°C before it will flower. If it is in lower temperatures
early in the year, flowering will be delayed. When the
last flower has faded, cut off the flower head with the
seed pods. Allow the hollow stem to wither naturally
and then remove it.

PROBLEM

Has the foliage turned yellow in early autumn?

IF YES

CAUSE This is entirely natural.
ACTION If it does not do so, in readiness for the
dormant period, force it to happen by witholding
water. When the leaves have withered, cut them off
and store the bulb completely dry in its compost at
50°F/10°C. In late winter, as new growth emerges,
remove the bulb from its pot, gently tease out old
compost, leave the old roots on, and repot with the
bulb shoulder showing above the compost. Bring it
into 65-70°F/18-21°C. Water the compost, gradually
giving water more frequently. Sometimes the flower
stem emerges first, and the plant may be in flower
before the leaves appear. Sometimes the leaves and
stem appear together, or the leaves may come first.
As long as it flowers, this hardly matters.

PROBLEM

Are the tips of the leaflets turning brown, or are whole fronds turning brown and dropping?

Howea forsteriana
The kentia palm comes from temperate wooded areas of Lord Howe Island, northwest of New Zealand. Summers are warm, 65-80°F/18-27°C, winters mild, 60°F/16°C. Rain falls evenly throughout the year. The palm has erect fronds of deeply divided dark green leaflets held on long stems, which arch over as they mature.

IF YES

CAUSE The air in the room is too dry. This is most likely to happen in a centrally heated room in winter.
ACTION Increase the humidity: see page 8.

IF NO

Are the tips of the fronds touching the wall?

IF YES

CAUSE Wall plaster is extremely absorbent; when the air is dry, it will draw moisture from any source, especially any leaves that touch the wall.
ACTION Move the plant away from the wall. If the brown tips look unsightly, they can be cut off, but do not cut into the green tissue of the leaflet or that, in turn, will go brown and so on along the leaflet.

IF NO

If you push a finger into the compost, is it dry well below the surface?

IF YES

CAUSE The compost has been allowed to dry out.
ACTION Water thoroughly until water runs out of the drainage hole in the pot. Thereafter, follow the watering routine in **IDEAL CONDITIONS**. Remove any completely brown fronds.

IF NO

Is the plant near a radiator or fire?

IF YES

CAUSE Overheating.
ACTION Move the plant to a place where the temperature is as near the ideal 55-65°/13-18°C as possible.

IF NO

Do people constantly brush past the plant?

IF YES

CAUSE Too much of the wrong kind of human contact.
ACTION Move it to a part of the room where it will be more out of the way.

IDEAL CONDITIONS

Temperature 55-65°F/13-18°C all year; rest the palm in winter not lower than 55°F/13°C.
Light Bright, but not direct sun. Tolerates some shade.
Water Twice a week in summer, so compost is always moist but never waterlogged. In winter, every seven to ten days.
Feed Every two weeks, late spring to early autumn.
Pot-on Every second spring in loam-based compost.
Propagation Sow seed in spring; bottom heat of 75-80°F/24-27°C is needed. Germination takes many months.

Hoya carnosa
Hoyas are trailing or climbing plants from the tropical rain forest areas of northern Australia. The climate is humid and warm, 70-85F/21-30°C all year. Summer and autumn can be very wet, but in winter little rain falls. Leaves are dark green, glossy and elliptical. White to pink flowers with red centres in summer – very fragrant.

IDEAL CONDITIONS

Temperature In summer 60-65°F/16-18°C. Rest the plant in winter at 50-55°F/10-13°C. Needs humidity.
Light Bright, with direct sun, except when it is fierce.
Water In summer, once or twice a week, but let the compost dry out a little between waterings. In winter, every 10 to 14 days.
Feed Every two weeks, late spring to early autumn.
Pot-on Every other year in spring in a peat- or loam-based compost.
Propagation Take stem cuttings in summer. Need a temperature of 70°F/21°C to root.

PROBLEM

Have the flower buds dropped, and has the plant failed to produce as many flowers as previously?

IF YES

CAUSE The most obvious one is that the plant has been moved from one place to another in the room.
ACTION Nothing can be done in the current year, but next year, leave the plant where it is as soon as the buds start developing.

IF NO

When the flowers faded the previous year did you cut off the whole flowering spur?

IF YES

CAUSE Cutting off the spurs means that no flowers can grow at that point again.
ACTION As flowers fade, let the flower and stalk fall of their own accord. If you must tidy up the plant, pick off flowers and short stalks only, not spurs.

PROBLEM

Are the leaves dry and curling and covered with papery brown spots?

IF YES

CAUSE The air is too dry.
ACTION Increase humidity by spraying the plant daily, but not when it is in flower; see also page 8.

IF NO

Has the plant been in hot sun for long periods?

IF YES

CAUSE The leaves have been scorched.
ACTION Remove any badly affected leaves. In future give the plant some direct sun, but not when fierce.

PROBLEM

Is the plant out of control, with long sprawling stems?

IF YES

CAUSE The natural vigorous growth of the plant, which will put on 18in/45cm a year or more.
ACTION Do not prune the stems or you will lose more flowers. Train them around a large hoop of wire or up a wooden framework.

PROBLEM

Are the leaves falling, and does the plant look dull and lifeless? If you push a finger into the compost is it dry?

IF YES

CAUSE Underwatering; the compost has dried out.
ACTION Water the compost thoroughly. If any of the stems are nearly bare, cut them back to 4in/10cm; new growth will soon appear. In future, follow the watering advice in **IDEAL CONDITIONS**.

IF NO

Has the plant been in an unheated room in winter?

IF YES

CAUSE The plant has been too cold.
ACTION Move it to a room where the temperature is 60°F/16°C or higher, never below 55°F/13°C.

IF NO

Is the air in the room dry?

IF YES

CAUSE Lack of humidity.
ACTION Spray the plants daily, or even more often in periods of very hot dry weather.

IF NO

Are there small black flies and tiny white maggots on the surface of the compost?

IF YES

CAUSE The black flies are fungus gnats, whose maggots feed on plant debris in wet compost and on roots. They can cause the total collapse of a plant.
ACTION Water the compost with diazinon or malathion and repeat every few days until the pests have gone. Then water less often, as in **IDEAL CONDITIONS**.

PROBLEM

Have the stems become bare and straggly?

IF YES

CAUSE This is the habit of the plant.
ACTION In winter cut back the stems to 4in/10cm. When new growth is well established, pinch out growing tips to encourage bushiness. Plants will not suffer if they are cut back two or three times a year.

Hypoestes sanguinolenta
Hypoestes comes from tropical rain forest areas of Madagascar. Temperature is 70-80°F/21-27°C all year, with constant high humidity and plenty of rain. However, strains of the plant have been bred which do not require such demanding conditions. The dark green oval leaves have pink spots or splashes.

IDEAL CONDITIONS

Temperature In summer, 65-70°F/ 18-21°C. Rest the plant in winter at about 60°F/16°C, but no lower than 55°F/13°C.
Light Bright, with some direct but not fierce sun. In shade, leaf colour will fade.
Water Two or three times a week in summer to keep compost always moist. Once a week in winter; let surface dry out a little before watering again.
Feed Every two weeks, late spring to early autumn.
Pot-on In spring in peat-based compost.
Propagation Take stem cuttings in summer; they need 70°F/21°C to root.

Impatiens wallerana
Impatiens originated in the temperate rain forests of East Africa, but many striking hybrids have now been developed from the humble Busy Lizzie. Year-round temperatures are 55-70°F/13-21°C; there is no dry season. Stems are fleshy, leaves bright green and flowers, from spring to autumn, pink, red, orange or white.

IDEAL CONDITIONS

Temperature 60-65°F/16-18°C all year; but in winter keep the plant at the lower end of the scale, and even down to 55°F/13°C.
Light Bright, but out of direct sun.
Water In summer, two or three times a week; in hot weather they can be thirsty plants. In winter, every 7 to 10 days.
Feed Every month from spring to early autumn.
Pot-on In spring in peat-based compost.
Propagation Sow seed in spring or take cuttings in summer. Cuttings may be planted straight into peat compost or rooted in water first.

PROBLEM

Are the leaves wilting and flowers falling? Does the compost feel dry just below the surface when you push in your finger?

IF YES

CAUSE Underwatering. If the compost has dried out completely, the leaves will wilt and the flowers fall.
ACTION The impatiens is a resilient plant and watering thoroughly will usually revive the plant. In hot weather daily watering may be necessary.

IF NO

Are the leaves and stems covered with fine white webs and white powder?

IF YES

CAUSE Red spider mites attracted by dry warmth.
ACTION Spray the plant with liquid derris and repeat every few days while the pests persist. Increase ventilation in the room and humidity: see page 8.

IF NO

Are the leaves also falling?

IF YES

CAUSE The temperature is too low.
ACTION Move the plant to a room with a temperature of 60-65°F/16-18°C and never below 55°F/13°C.

PROBLEM

Has the plant refused to flower and is growth generally weak and spindly?

IF YES

CAUSE Not enough light.
ACTION Move the plant closer to a window where it will get bright light but not direct sunlight. Prune all spindly stems to within 6in/15cm of the compost. This is best done in spring and early summer.

PROBLEM

Are the stems rotting at the base?

IF YES

CAUSE Overwatering; more likely in winter.
ACTION Remove rotting stems. Dust the compost with fungicide powder and let it dry out; then follow watering instructions in **IDEAL CONDITIONS**.

PROBLEM

Do the leaves look dull, with brown edges? Is the whole plant generally lifeless? Has it failed to flower?

IF YES

CAUSE The air is too dry. In temperatures above 60°F/16°C the plant needs constant humidity.
ACTION Create a humid atmosphere around the plant: see page 8. Mist spray daily in warm weather.

IF NO

Has the plant been in a shaded part of the room?

IF YES

CAUSE Lack of light affects flowering.
ACTION Move the plant closer to a window where the light is always bright, with direct sun. A jacobinia needs protecting only from fierce midday sun.

IF NO

If you push a finger into the compost does it feel dry about 2in/5cm below the surface?

IF YES

CAUSE The plant has had too little water.
ACTION Water it thoroughly, letting excess water run away through the drainage hole in the pot. Follow watering instructions in **IDEAL CONDITIONS** in future.

PROBLEM

Has the plant grown straggly, with bare lower stems?

IF YES

CAUSE Jacobinias naturally grow like this and look good for two years at the most. It is then best to start with new plants.
ACTION If the plant is only in its second year, cut down bare stems, if they are few, to within 4in/10cm of the compost and pinch out the growing tips of well-established new shoots for bushiness. After two years, replace plants by stem cuttings in spring.

OTHER SPECIES

Jacobinia pauciflora has small, bright green oval leaves and clusters of tubular red flowers with yellow tips in late autumn.

Jacobinia carnea
Jacobinia is an evergreen shrub from the warm rain forest areas of Brazil. The temperature all year is 75°C/24°C and rainfall is plentiful and constant. Jacobinias are short-lived plants indoors, for they fairly soon begin to look unattractive. Oval, glossy, dark green leaves; plume-shaped, pink to red flowers in late summer.

IDEAL CONDITIONS

Temperature In summer 60-65°F/16-18°C. Rest the plant in winter at about 55°F/13°C. Needs humidity when the weather is hot.
Light Bright, direct sun all year, except when it is scorching.
Water In summer, twice a week to keep compost always moist. In winter, once a week, to prevent the compost from drying out.
Feed Every two weeks from late spring to early autumn.
Pot-on Only once, hardly worthwhile.
Propagation Replace plants by stem cuttings every spring in peat-based compost.

Jasminum polyanthum
This jasmine is a vigorous flowering climber from forest areas of China with hot summers, 75°F/24°C, and winters, around 55°F/13°C. Rain falls year round but is heaviest in spring and summer. The dark green leaves are made up of six leaflets on branching stems; fragrant white flowers bloom in winter and spring.

IDEAL CONDITIONS

Temperature In summer ideally around 60°F/16°C. In winter a maximum of 55°F/13°C.
Light Bright, with direct sunlight, but shade the plant from very hot sun.
Water Two or three times a week in summer to keep the compost always moist. In winter, about once a week; allow the surface of the compost to dry out slightly before watering again.
Feed Every two weeks from late spring to early autumn.
Pot-on In summer in loam-based compost.
Propagation Take stem cuttings in summer.

PROBLEM

Are the leaves curling, drying up and falling? Have the flower buds turned brown and failed to open?

IF YES

CAUSE The room is too warm and too dry.
ACTION Move the plant to a room where the temperature is no higher than 55°F/13°C. Regularly spray the foliage, except when the plant is in flower for you then risk marking the petals.

IF NO

When you push a finger into the compost does it feel dry about 2in/5cm below the surface?

IF YES

CAUSE Underwatering.
ACTION Water the compost thoroughly, then follow the watering instructions in **IDEAL CONDITIONS**.

IF NO

Has the plant been in a shady part of the room?

IF YES

CAUSE Not enough light. In poor light, flower buds often do not open and may not even form.
ACTION Put the plant nearer a window where it will get direct sun. Shade only from the strongest sun.

IF NO

Has the plant been in a sunny spot, with no shade?

IF YES

CAUSE This time it is overexposure to hot sunlight, which has scorched the leaves.
ACTION Either move the plant to a place near the window in which the sun will fall on it only in the morning or late afternoon, or shade it from hot sun.

PROBLEM

Is the plant producing sprawling stems several feet long after flowering and getting out of control?

IF YES

CAUSE This is the way the plant grows.
ACTION After flowering, cut back all stems to within 6in/15cm of the compost. When the new stems are long enough, train them around a wire hoop.

PROBLEM

Do the fleshy leaves look bloated, and have they started to rot?

IF YES

CAUSE Overwatering. The leaves are able to store water for use in time of drought. If the compost is kept permanently wet, instead of just moist, the plant will continue to draw up moisture, and the leaves will swell and may rot.
ACTION Remove all completely rotted leaves. Dust the compost with fungicide powder and let it dry out. Then water as in **IDEAL CONDITIONS**. If all the leaves are rotting, throw the plant away.

IF NO

Are the leaves also covered with brown and yellow damp spots?

IF YES

CAUSE This is leaf spot disease, caused by overwatering, or watering on to the leaves, and poor ventilation.
ACTION Remove badly marked leaves and spray with benomyl. Thereafter water as in **IDEAL CONDITIONS** and increase ventilation.

PROBLEM

Have the leaves started to shrivel?

IF YES

CAUSE Underwatering; this is most likely to happen in winter. The compost has dried out, and the leaves have used up their reserves of water.
ACTION Water thoroughly and ensure the compost does not dry out again.

PROBLEM

In its second year has the plant flowered poorly or not at all?

IF YES

CAUSE The kalanchoë is what is known as a short-day plant and needs restricted light to form flower buds.
ACTION In mid-autumn, put the plant in a room in which it will get 10 hours of daylight and 14 hours of complete darkness for eight weeks. Then return it to a sunny spot and flower buds should soon appear. The plant is usually not worth keeping after two years.

Kalanchoë blossfeldiana
Kalanchoë is a succulent native to Madagascar, where temperatures are 70-80°F/21-27°C all year with most rain in the hottest period. The plant copes with the months of little or no rain by storing water in its fleshy dark green leaves. Clusters of tiny yellow, orange or red flowers appear from early winter to spring.

IDEAL CONDITIONS

Temperature In summer 60-65°F/16-18°C.. Give the plant a winter rest at 55-60°F/13-16°C.
Light Bright, direct sun all the year, except, when fierce.
Water About once a week in summer so the compost is just moist. Every 10 to 14 days in winter to prevent the compost drying out completely.
Feed Every three or four weeks from late spring to early autumn.
Pot-on In spring in loam-based compost; the plant is, however, often discarded after its second year.
Propagation Take stem cuttings or sow seed in spring.

L I L I U M

Lilium longiflorum
The Easter Lily is a flowering bulb native to Japan. Temperatures reach 75°F/24°C in summer; in winter, 40-50°F/5-10°C. Rainfall is plentiful all year. Tall stems, with narrow, dark green pointed leaves, bear large white trumpet-shaped flowers with orange stamens in late spring and early summer. They last only a short time.

IDEAL CONDITIONS

Temperature For early flowering, put the bulb in a temperature of 60°F/16°C in early spring. Wait a little longer for later flowering. In winter, keep the bulb at around 40°F/5°C.
Light Bright, but no direct sunlight.
Water Once or twice a week when starting into growth. After flowering, once a week. When bulb is stored in a cold spot, about once a month.
Feed Every two weeks after growth appears until flowering ends.
Pot-on In loam-based compost after stem has withered.
Propagation By off-sets when potting-on.

◁ PROBLEM ▷

After flowering, have stem and leaves turned yellow, started to wither and die down?

── IF YES ──

CAUSE This is the natural life cycle of the plant, but it may be worth saving the bulb for a second year.
ACTION When the stem has withered completely, pull it away from the bulb. Remove the bulb from the pot and gently tease compost from the roots, damaging them as little as possible. Pot in fresh compost with 1in/2.5cm of gravel in the bottom of the pot for good drainage; set the base of the bulb half-way down the pot. Keep the pot in a good light at around 40°F/5°C and frost-free. Watering once a month should be sufficient, but do not let the compost dry out. Start feeding the bulb when shoots appear. The result may be disappointing – less vigorous growth and small flowers – so after a year inside you may prefer to plant the bulb outside to flower in the garden in future.

── IF NO ──

Has the stem started to wither before flowering?

── IF YES ──

CAUSE The bulb is probably rotting due to overwatering.
ACTION Scrape away the compost until the bulb is visible. Press it gently; if it feels soft and mushy rot has set in. Throw the bulb away, for nothing else can be done. In future, water as in **IDEAL CONDITIONS**.

── PROBLEM ──

Has the plant failed to flower or produced buds which have not opened?

── IF YES ──

CAUSE The plant has not had enough light.
ACTION Nothing is possible if there are no flower buds. Putting the plant in a good light at this stage will not induce it to flower, but try again next year, giving it good light. Plants in bud should be moved to a bright but sunless window to induce the buds to open.

OTHER SPECIES
Lilium tigrinum has deep orange to red petals with purple-black spots and dark red pollen.

PROBLEM

Have the leaves begun to shrivel, when flowering is over and you have stopped watering?

IF YES

CAUSE This is the natural growth cycle of the plant. The leaves shrivel and will eventually die altogether, but they will be replaced by new pairs of leaves. These may not emerge until spring.

ACTION None. Do not attempt to remove shrivelling leaves because by doing so you are likely to damage those which are developing. Only when leaves have shrivelled and are loose should they be removed.

IF NO

Are the leaves shrivelling at other times of the year, in summer in particular?

IF YES

CAUSE Underwatering. The fleshy leaves store water. If the compost dries out altogether, the plant will turn to this supply, and when it is used up the leaves will begin to shrivel.

ACTION Water the compost thoroughly. The plant is best watered from below to avoid the leaves rotting. Place the pot in about 2in/5cm of water for about 30 minutes, then allow excess water to drain away. Thereafter water as advised in **IDEAL CONDITIONS**.

PROBLEM

Has the plant failed to flower?

IF YES

CAUSE Not enough light.

ACTION Move the plant to a windowsill where it will get direct sun all year round, especially in winter.

PROBLEM

Do the leaves look bloated and feel soft?

IF YES

CAUSE With cacti and succulents, this is a sure sign of overwatering.

ACTION Allow the compost to dry out and then follow watering instructions in **IDEAL CONDITIONS**. The leaves may also have started to rot. Drying out the compost may give the plant a chance, but if the rot is already far gone the plant should be discarded.

Lithops lesliei
The lithops is an unusual succulent from arid bush areas of South Africa. Summers are fairly dry and warm (70°F/21°C), winters quite wet and mild (50-55°F/10-13°C). At least half of the single pair of fleshy grey-green leaves, spotted reddish-brown, is buried in the soil as protection against sun and wind. Yellow flowers in autumn.

IDEAL CONDITIONS

Temperature Normal warm summer room temperatures and hot weather suit this plant. Rest it in winter at about 50°F/10°C.
Light Very bright, with direct sun always.
Water Once a week in summer; let the compost almost dry out before watering again. Do not water into the slit dividing the leaves. When flowering ends, stop watering. Start again when new growth begins.
Feed Monthly, spring to early autumn.
Pot-on Every two or three years in half loam-based compost, half sand.
Propagation Divide or sow seed in spring.

Lobivia hertrichiana
Lobivia is a desert cactus native to Bolivia (its name is an anagram) and Peru. Temperatures by day are up to 100°F/38°C, with ground frost at night. Rainfall is limited to short, sharp showers. The fleshy globular stems, each with several ribs edged with brown spines, store water against drought. Scarlet flowers appear in summer.

IDEAL CONDITIONS

Temperature This cactus can cope with normal room temperatures in summer as well as very warm weather. In winter, rest the plant at 45°F/7°C.
Light Bright with direct sun all year. It is most important in winter when the plant is building itself up for flowering.
Water Twice a week in summer to keep compost always moist. Once a week in winter.
Feed Every two weeks, late spring to early autumn.
Pot-on Every two or three years in spring in loam-based compost plus sand.
Propagation By offsets when potting-on.

PROBLEM

Are the brown spines on the edges of the ribs of the cactus paling to yellow?

IF YES

CAUSE This is not a problem but an advantage, for it means that the cactus is getting plenty of sunlight. It can usually be taken as a sign that the plant will flower well, since successful flowering depends upon adequate sunlight.
ACTION Simply wait for the flowers to appear.

PROBLEM

Has the plant failed to flower?

IF YES

CAUSE During the winter it has had insufficient sunlight and has been kept too warm.
ACTION Next winter make sure that the plant has a rest at 45°F/7°C, but it should also get as much sun as possible. When the plant does produce flowers, they open in the daytime and close again at night.

PROBLEM

Are there white woolly patches on the stems?

IF YES

CAUSE The plant is being attacked by mealy bugs, which hide in these fluffy cocoons and leave unsightly patches where they have sucked the sap.
ACTION Spray the stems with water to dislodge the insects. In bad infestations, spray with liquid derris and repeat every few days until the pests have gone.

PROBLEM

Are the stems beginning to shrivel?

IF YES

CAUSE Not enough water; most likely in winter when watering is limited. Checking once a week to see whether the compost is too dry lessens the risk. The spines may prevent your pushing a finger into the compost; instead lift the pot to see how light (dry) or heavy (moist) it is. Practice is needed, and it is easier to judge with plastic pots than with clay.
ACTION Water the plant from underneath by standing it in 2in/5cm of water for 30 minutes. Allow excess to drain away before returning the pot to its saucer.

PROBLEM

Are the spines dull in colour? Has the cactus failed to flower? Has it been in a shady part of the room?

Mammillaria bocasana

Mammillaria is a good cactus for the beginner since it flowers well when young. Its home is the Mexican desert, where temperatures soar to 100°F/38°C by day and drop to freezing at night; rainfall is low. The cactus stores water in its blue-green globes, covered in small spiny tubercules. Creamy flowers bloom in spring.

==== IF YES ====

CAUSE Not enough light, especially direct sunlight.
ACTION Move the plant to a windowsill which gets bright light with direct sun all year round. This is doubly important in winter.

==== IF NO ====

Has the cactus been in a centrally heated room throughout the winter?

==== IF YES ====

CAUSE The plant has been denied the winter rest it needs to encourage it to flower.
ACTION None immediately, but in late autumn or early winter move the plant to an unheated room with a temperature as low as 45°F/7°C. Good light and direct sun are still needed.

==== IF NO ====

Do the bases of the stems also feel soft and mushy, and are they turning brown?

==== IF YES ====

CAUSE The stems are rotting because of overwatering or watering between the clumps of stems.
ACTION If all the stems are rotting, there is nothing to do but throw the cactus away. If only a few are affected, cut those away, dust the compost with fungicide powder and let the compost dry out. Then follow the watering instructions in **IDEAL CONDITIONS**. If the pots are full of stems, water around the outside edge of the clump. Better still, let the pot stand in about 2in/5cm of water for 30 minutes. Let the excess water drain away before putting the pot back on its saucer.

OTHER SPECIES

Mammillaria elegans has cylindrical stems, covered with short white spines, and red flowers.
Mammillaria zeilmanniana has elongated globes covered with whitish-brown spines; red flowers encircle the top of the globe.

IDEAL CONDITIONS

Temperature In summer, usual room temperatures or warmer are all right. In winter 45°F/7°C.
Light Bright, with full direct sun all year.
Water Twice a week in summer; let surface dry out a little before watering again. In winter about once a month so compost does not dry out altogether.
Feed Monthly, from spring to early autumn.
Pot-on In spring in two-thirds loam-based compost and one-third sand.
Propagation Remove offsets when potting-on. If there are few roots, let the offsets dry out for a day or two before potting.

Maranta leuconeura
'Kerchoveana'
Marantas originate in
tropical rain forests of
Central and South
America which are hot,
75-80°F/24-27°C, and
humid. Rain is plentiful
all year. At night, the
oval leaves of the plant
become erect, and fold
together in pairs,
displaying their grey
undersides. New leaves
have dark brown
markings that later turn
dark green.

IDEAL CONDITIONS

Temperature In
summer, 65-70°F/
18-21°C. Rest the
plant in winter at
60-65°F/16-18°C. It
should never be kept
below 55°F/13°C.
Humidity is needed
Light Bright, but no
direct sun.
Water Two or three
times a week in
summer, so the
compost is always
moist. Once a week
in winter; it must
never be allowed to
dry out completely.
Feed Every two
weeks, late spring to
early autumn.
Pot-on In spring in a
peat-based compost.
Propagation Divide
when potting-on.
Each clump should
have enough roots to
support growth.

PROBLEM

Are the tips of the leaves turning brown and
brittle? Is the plant in a warm, centrally heated
room?

IF YES

CAUSE The air is too dry.
ACTION Create a humid atmosphere: see page 8. A
daily mist spray will help, especially in warm weather.

IF NO

Has the plant been on or near a sunny windowsill?

IF YES

CAUSE Direct sun, which has scorched the leaves.
ACTION Move the plant to a position where it will get
good light but no direct sun. Cut off any badly marked
leaves at compost level.

IF NO

When you push a finger into the compost does it feel
dry about 2in/5cm below the surface?

IF YES

CAUSE Underwatering.
ACTION Water the compost, allowing any excess to
drain away from the hole in the bottom of the pot. In
future, follow the watering instructions given in **IDEAL
CONDITIONS**.

IF NO

Has the plant been in an unheated room in winter?

IF YES

CAUSE It has been too cold for the plant.
ACTION Move the plant to a room with a minimum temperature of 55°F/13°C. The ideal range is 60-65°F/
16-18°C.

PROBLEM

In winter, are the leaves turning brown, curling and
dying?

IF YES

CAUSE This is natural. It will happen over a period of
time and the plant may die down altogether.
ACTION When the leaves have completely withered,
cut them away at compost level. Continue to water the
compost, and in spring new growth will appear.

PROBLEM

Are the frond tips turning brown and brittle and whole fronds shrivelling? Is the plant in a centrally heated room?

IF YES

CAUSE The air is too dry.
ACTION Provide a humid atmosphere in the immediate area of the plant by standing the pot on a tray of wet pebbles or surrounding it with moist peat. Mist spray the leaves daily, especially in periods of warm weather. Use rainwater if possible; hard mains water contains lime, which leaves unsightly white deposits on the fronds. Brown tips can be cut off, but do not cut into the green tissue; this is the quickest way to turn the whole leaflet brown.

IF NO

When you push a finger into the compost does it feel dry about 2in/5cm below the surface?

IF YES

CAUSE Underwatering. The compost has been allowed to dry out.
ACTION Water the compost thoroughly until excess water runs out of the drainage hole in the bottom of the pot. If the compost is so dry it has shrunk from the side of the pot, water will escape through the gap and the compost will not become moist. If this is the case, put the pot in a bucket of water with the water almost up to the rim but not over it. Leave for about 30 minutes until the water has penetrated the compost ball and it is thoroughly moist. (At this point, you can see beads of moisture on the surface of the compost.) Remove any completely shrivelled fronds. Use soft water – rainwater or distilled water – whenever possible, since hard water contains lime, which can also cause the fronds to turn brown.

IF NO

Has the plant been in an unheated room in winter?

IF YES

CAUSE The temperature is too low.
ACTION Move the plant to a heated room with a minimum temperature of 60°F/16°C; a little higher is better in these circumstances. This palm also needs spring and summer temperatures of 65-70°F/18-21°C if it is to put on healthy new growth.

Microcoelum weddellianum
The coconut palm leads a well regulated life in the tropical rain forests of Brazil. Temperatures are a constant 75-80°F/24-27°C. Rain falls almost every day, and the air is always moist. Indoors, a young 12-in/30-cm specimen will take many years to reach some 5ft/1.5m, which is about its limit. Extremely delicate fronds.

IDEAL CONDITIONS

Temperature In summer, 65-70°F/18-21°C. Rest the palm in winter at 60-65°F/16-18°C. Needs humidity.
Light Bright, but no direct sun.
Water Twice a week in summer so the compost is moist all the time. Once a week in winter.
Feed Every two weeks from late spring to early autumn.
Pot-on Every other year in spring in loam-based compost. Treat roots gently, they are easily damaged.
Propagation Sow seed in spring; it will be a long time before the palm reaches a decent size.

Miltonia vexillaria
Miltonias are native to Columbia. They grow at altitudes up to 6,000 ft/ 1,800 m, with an average temperature of 60-70°F/16-21°C and rain all year. At the highest altitudes, it is cooler and less wet. Leaves are bright green and strap-shaped. Pansy-like flowers, pink to red with yellow markings, bloom in late spring.

IDEAL CONDITIONS

Temperature In summer, 65-70°F/ 18-21°C by day; 65°F/18°C at night. In winter, 60-65°F/16-18°C by day and 60°F/16°C at night. The orchid needs humidity.
Light Bright, but no direct sun.
Water Twice a week in summer to keep compost moist, not waterlogged. Once a week in winter to stop it drying out.
Feed Monthly, spring to late autumn.
Pot-on After flowering, in an orchid compost.
Propagation Divide the rhizome when potting-on. There must be two or more pseudobulbs to each piece of the rhizome.

PROBLEM

Are the tips of the leaves turning brown, and has the plant failed to flower? Is the plant in a dry warm room?

IF YES

CAUSE Lack of humidity.
ACTION Create a humid atmosphere: see page 8. In very warm weather mist spray the plant daily.

IF NO

Are there soft brown spots on the leaves?

IF YES

CAUSE Leaf spot disease, encouraged by excessive humidity. At lower temperatures the plant does not require such a high degree of humidity.
ACTION Any badly affected leaves should be removed. Spray with benomyl. Increase ventilation and stop mist spraying until the disease disappears.

IF NO

Has the plant been in a shaded part of the room?

IF YES

CAUSE Not enough light. Plants will not flower in poor light.
ACTION Move the plant closer to a window where it will get bright light but no direct sun. Good light is specially important in winter when the plant is building itself up for flowering.

IF NO

Are the leaves also covered with a white powder?

IF YES

CAUSE Mildew, again encouraged by excessive humidity and poor ventilation.
ACTION Badly affected leaves should be removed. Spray with benomyl and increase ventilation.

PROBLEM

Is the foliage turning pale and does it appear bleached out? Has the plant been in a sunny window?

IF YES

CAUSE Direct sun, which has scorched the foliage.
ACTION Move the plant to a position where it will have bright light but no direct sun.

PROBLEM

Are the leaf tips turning brown and papery? Are some leaves turning yellow and dying? Does the compost feel dry about 2in/5cm down?

IF YES

CAUSE Underwatering.
ACTION Thoroughly water the compost until excess water flows from the drainage hole in the bottom of the pot. In future follow watering instructions in IDEAL CONDITIONS. The brown tips may be trimmed but do not cut into the green leaf tissue for this will accelerate the browning. In the wild, the plant takes up moisture and food by means of its aerial roots. They can be stuck into the compost, but fill the pot rapidly, denying the underground roots room to develop. Rather train the roots around a moss stick, kept constantly moist.

IF NO

When you push a finger into the compost does it feel wet and sodden?

IF YES

CAUSE Overwatering, especially in winter, has water-logged the compost. Another sign of overwatering is when excess water is expelled from the leaf edges.
ACTION Allow the compost to dry out and then water as in IDEAL CONDITIONS. Remove any completely yellow leaves, with their stalks, from the main stem.

IF NO

Is only the lowest leaf turning yellow?

IF YES

CAUSE Entirely natural. As the plant ages, so leaves fall, starting with the lowest one.
ACTION When the leaf is completely yellow, cut it away, with the stalk, from the main stem.

PROBLEM

Are the new leaves small with fewer incisions and is the plant becoming leggy? Are variegated forms losing their colouring?

IF YES

CAUSE Not enough light, resulting in stunted poor growth and variegated leaves turning plain green.
ACTION Move the plant to a position where it will get bright light all year round but no direct sun.

Monstera deliciosa
The Swiss cheese plant is a native of tropical rain forests of Central America. Temperatures all year are 70-75°F/ 21-24°C; rainfall is plentiful. It is also found in cooler, higher areas. To support the heavy, thick stem and slashed, perforated dark green leaves, the plant clings to tree trunks with its aerial roots.

IDEAL CONDITIONS

Temperature 65-75°F/21-24°C all year, but down to 55°F/13°C is tolerated.
Light Bright, but not direct sun. Plants with variegated leaves need good light at all times to keep their colouring.
Water Once a week in summer, more often in very hot weather. In winter, every 7 to 10 days should be enough.
Feed Every two weeks from late spring to early autumn.
Pot-on In spring in a loam-based compost.
Propagation Take stem cuttings in summer or sow seed in spring.

MONSTERA

Neoregelia carolinae 'Tricolor'
Neoregelia is an epiphytic bromeliad from the warm (75-80°F/24-27°C.) tropical rain forests of Brazil. It clings by its roots to branches of trees. The toothed, shiny green leaves, striped yellow, form a rosette. In the forest, water collects in the central vase; indoors it must be topped up when the plant is in growth.

IDEAL CONDITIONS

Temperature In summer, 65-70°F/18-21°C. Rest the plant in winter at 55-60°F/13-16°C, but no lower.
Light Bright, with some sun for good colour, but shade plants from fierce sunlight.
Water Once, possibly twice, a week in summer. Keep central rosette topped up with water. In winter every 7 to 10 days and keep the rosette dry.
Feed Monthly, spring to late autumn.
Pot-on Every other year in spring in peat-based compost.
Propagation Remove offsets from the base of the parent plant.

PROBLEM

Are the leaves turning brown and shrivelling?

IF YES

CAUSE The air is too dry.
ACTION Provide humidity: see page 8.

IF NO

When you push a finger into the compost does it feel dry about 2in/5cm down?

IF YES

CAUSE Underwatering.
ACTION Water the compost until excess water flows from the hole in the bottom of the pot. Fill the central rosette with water and top it up regularly. Thereafter follow watering instructions in **IDEAL CONDITIONS**.

PROBLEM

Is the main plant dying down after flowering?

IF YES

CAUSE Entirely natural; it may take a long time.
ACTION If it begins to look unattractive, cut the plant away, leaving the offsets to develop, or detach the offsets and repot in fresh compost. Offsets should be at least 4-5in/10-12.5cm tall, with several leaves.

IF NO

Is the base of the plant turning brown and does it feel soft and mushy?

IF YES

CAUSE The plant is rotting through overwatering and being kept in too low a temperature. This can happen in winter when plants need to be kept fairly dry.
ACTION It may be too late to save the plant, but drying out may revive it. If not, throw it away.

PROBLEM

Has the centre of the rosette started to turn red?

IF YES

CAUSE This is entirely natural and denotes the onset of flowering.
ACTION None. The flowers are short-lived, but the red colouring will last for many months.

N E P H R O L E P I S

⬦ **PROBLEM** ⬦

Are the fronds turning brown and shrivelling? If you push a finger into the compost, does it feel dry about 2in/5cm down?

──── **IF YES** ────

CAUSE Underwatering. The soil ball has been allowed to dry out.

ACTION Water the compost thoroughly until water runs out of the drainage hole of the pot. However, the compost, especially if it is a peat-based compost, may have shrunk from the side of the pot and the water may simply run through the gap without wetting the compost. It is, therefore, better to immerse the pot in a pail of water and leave it for 30 minutes. Completely shrivelled fronds should be cut away at compost level. If all fronds are affected, cut them to within 2in/5cm of the compost. Spray this stubble frequently, keep the compost moist, and new growth should emerge—if the roots have not died

──── **IF NO** ────

Has the plant been in a dry, centrally heated room?

──── **IF YES** ────

CAUSE Lack of humidity.

ACTION Stand the pot on a tray of wet pebbles or surround it with moist peat. If the fern is in a hanging container, spray it daily, with soft water.

──── **PROBLEM** ────

Is the foliage turning yellow, with no new growth?

──── **IF YES** ────

CAUSE The nutrients in the compost are exhausted and have not been replaced by regular feeding.

ACTION Give fertilizers every two weeks from late spring to early autumn, following the maker's advice about dosage. Do not feed for the rest of the year.

──── **IF NO** ────

Are roots growing through the hole in the pot?

──── **IF YES** ────

CAUSE The roots have filled the pot and there is insufficient compost to hold the water and food that the plant needs for healthy growth.

ACTION Pot-on to a larger pot in fresh compost in spring or summer, never in winter.

Nephrolepis exaltata
The Boston fern grows in tropical rain forests from Florida to South America, where there is plenty of rain all year and warmth – 75-80°F/ 24-27°C. They may cover the ground or grow as epiphytes, their roots clinging to branches of trees. The many cultivars of the species all have fronds with opposite pairs of bright green pinnae.

IDEAL CONDITIONS

Temperature 55-65°F/13-18°C all year; but the fern benefits from a winter rest at 55-60°F/13-16°C.

Light Good, out of direct sun. Some shade tolerated.

Water Twice a week in summer so compost is not too dry. Once a week in winter; less often if in the cool.

Feed Every two weeks, late spring to early autumn.

Pot-on In spring in peat-based compost.

Propagation Divide when potting-on. Or else pin down the plantlets, which appear on runners, in peat-based compost. When rooted, sever from the main plant.

Nertera granadensis
Nertera is a creeping plant from New Zealand and parts of South America. Summer temperatures are 60-65°F/16-18°C those in winter 45-50°F/7-10°C, when most rain falls, although summers are not dry. The long stems have oval fleshy leaves. Small white flowers in spring and early summer become long-lasting orange berries.

IDEAL CONDITIONS

Temperature In summer 60°F/16°C is best, but the plant tolerates a higher temperature. In winter, 50°F/10°C.
Light Bright, with some direct sun all year.
Water Twice a week in summer so that the compost is always moist. In winter, every 7 to 10 days to stop compost from drying out completely.
Feed Monthly, spring to early autumn.
Pot-on In spring in peat-based compost with added sand. Use a shallow pot.
Propagation Divide when potting-on. Or sow seed in spring with 70°F/21°C bottom heat.

◁ PROBLEM ▷

Has the plant flowered and fruited poorly or produced no flowers or fruit, even though the foliage looks lush and healthy?

IF YES

CAUSE The plant has been too warm in spring and summer. Above 65°F/18°C, it tends to grow a mass of foliage at the expense of flowers and berries.
ACTION Nothing immediately. Keep the plant cool (50°F/10°C) during the next winter. In late spring put it outdoors in a sunny, sheltered spot, bring it in when the berries start to form. If it has to remain indoors, keep the temperature around 60°F/16°C and increase humidity: see page 8. Spray regularly.

IF NO

Has the plant been in a shady spot?

IF YES

CAUSE Not enough light. Nerteras need bright light with direct sunshine two or three hours a day.
ACTION Move the plant to a sunny windowsill.

IF NO

Has the plant been fed more often than advised in **IDEAL CONDITIONS**?

IF YES

CAUSE It has been overfed.
ACTION Cut the feeding to once a month from spring to early autumn and reduce the strength of the feed.

PROBLEM

Have the berries begun to fall after only a few weeks?

IF YES

CAUSE The plant has been too warm. It must be cool during the winter months if the berries are to last.
ACTION Move it to a cool room, about 50°F/10°C.

PROBLEM

Do the leaves look translucent?

IF YES

CAUSE The plant has been touched by frost; it will not tolerate a temperature below 40°F/5°C.
ACTION Move it into 50°F/10°C. If the roots have not been frostbitten, the plant may recover.

PROBLEM

Are leaf tips turning brown, and are there brown spots on the leaves? Has the plant failed to flower?

——————— **IF YES** ———————

CAUSE The air is too dry.
ACTION Create a humid atmosphere: see page 8. In warm weather mist spray regularly. Brown leaf tips may be cut off, but do not cut into the green tissue.

——————— **IF NO** ———————

Has the plant been kept in constantly warm temperatures in a centrally heated room?

——————— **IF YES** ———————

CAUSE Too much heat. Flowering will be affected if plants are always in temperatures above 70°F/21°C.
ACTION Move the plant to a room where the average temperature is about 60°F/16°C all year with a drop in temperature to 50°F/10°C at night.

——————— **IF NO** ———————

Has the plant been exposed to direct sunlight?

——————— **IF YES** ———————

CAUSE The sun has scorched the foliage, leaving hard dry brown spots.
ACTION Move the plant, so it gets bright light but no direct sun. Remove any badly affected leaves.

——————— **IF NO** ———————

Has the marking on the foliage occurred during the winter months?

——————— **IF YES** ———————

CAUSE Too much humidity, coupled with the lower temperatures.
ACTION Reduce the level of humidity around the plant. Drain water from pebble-filled trays and allow peat to dry out for a few days. Do not spray plants.

——————— **PROBLEM** ———————

Are the pseudobulbs shrivelling?

——————— **IF YES** ———————

CAUSE Insufficient water.
ACTION Water the compost thoroughly. It will take some time for the pseudobulbs to swell again.

Odontoglossum grande
This orchid is a native of Guatemala, found in cloud forest at high altitudes. 60-70°F/16-21°C by day, a little less at night. The air is always moist. Short pseudobulbs produce two bright green strap-shaped leaves. Large bright yellow flowers with reddish bands appear in autumn.

IDEAL CONDITIONS

Temperature In daytime 60°F/16°C all year, dropping to 50°F/10°C at night. Temperatures to 70°F/21°C tolerated by day, above is harmful. Requires humidity.
Light Bright, but no direct sun.
Water Twice a week in summer to keep compost moist. Once a week in winter; let compost almost dry out between waterings.
Feed Monthly, spring to early autumn.
Pot-on Every year, after flowering, in an orchid compost.
Propagation Divide the rhizome when potting-on; each piece must have four pseudobulbs or more.

Opuntia microdasys
The prickly pear comes from the Mexican desert, where day temperatures soar to 100°F/38°C and drop to freezing at night. Rain is unpredictable, falling in short, heavy downpours, and the plant stores water in its stems. These are fleshy, flattened, padlike and branching and are covered with yellow bristles.

IDEAL CONDITIONS

Temperature Normal room temperatures in summer—heat does not worry this cactus. Rest it in winter at 50-60°F/10-16°C, but not below 50°F/10°C.
Light Bright, with direct sun always.
Water Twice a week in summer, so compost is always moist. Once every two weeks or so during its winter rest.
Feed Every two weeks, late spring to early autumn.
Pot-on In spring in two-thirds loam-based compost to one-third sand.
Propagation Take cuttings in summer by removing a complete pad. Dry it out for a few days before potting.

PROBLEM

Are the stems covered with reddish-brown patches?

IF YES

CAUSE Too low temperature in winter. Patches will appear on the stems if they are kept below 50°F/10°C. Once marked, the pads will remain that way.
ACTION Move the plant to a room with a minimum temperature of 50°F/10°C; closer to 60°F/16°C is better.

IF NO

Are there also white woolly patches on the pads?

IF YES

CAUSE An infestation of mealy bugs, which suck the sap, leaving yellow patches that turn brown.
ACTION Gently wipe or brush away all traces of the insects taking care not to damage the bristles. Spray the plant with liquid derris. Repeat every few days if the insects persist.

IF NO

Do the patches feel soft?

IF YES

CAUSE Stem rot disease. This often follows an attack by mealy bugs, which excrete honeydew, so encouraging fungal diseases.
ACTION Cut away badly affected areas. Dust compost with a fungicide powder or soak it with benomyl.

PROBLEM

Have the pads started to shrivel and fall?

IF YES

CAUSE Underwatering
ACTION Water the compost thoroughly and in future water as in **IDEAL CONDITIONS**.

PROBLEM

Are the stems becoming elongated and losing their pad-like shape? Is the plant in a shaded part of the room?

IF YES

CAUSE Not enough light. Too much warmth in winter.
ACTION Move to a bright window. The temperature should be no higher than 60°F/16°C in winter.

P A C H Y S T A C H Y S

PROBLEM

Are flowers and leaves falling? Has the plant failed to flower? Is the air in the room dry?

─── **IF YES** ───

CAUSE Lack of humidity. Plants will not flower without adequate humidity, and those that do bloom will rapidly lose their flowers and bracts in a dry, badly ventilated room.
ACTION Provide humidity: see page 8. Mist spray the plant, but not when it is in flower since water will mark both flowers and bracts.

─── **IF NO** ───

When you push a finger into the compost does it feel dry about 2in/5cm down?

─── **IF YES** ───

CAUSE Underwatering.
ACTION Thoroughly water the compost. If the compost has shrunk from the side of the pot, immerse it in water to within about 2in/5cm of the rim for about 30 minutes until moisture can be seen on the surface.

─── **IF NO** ───

Has the plant been in an unheated room?

─── **IF YES** ───

CAUSE The temperature is too low.
ACTION Move the plant to a room with a temperature of 55-60°F/13-16°C.

─── **IF NO** ───

Is the plant in a shaded part of the room?

─── **IF YES** ───

CAUSE The plant is not getting enough light. It must have bright light at all times if it is to flower. This is especially important in winter when the plant is building up to flowering the following year.

─── **PROBLEM** ───

Is the plant growing too big and getting out of hand?

─── **IF YES** ───

CAUSE Natural growth, but it can be controlled.
ACTION In spring, prune stems to 6in/15cm or over-long stems to the same height as the others.

Pachystachys lutea
The lollipop plant comes from high forested areas of Peru that are warm all year (60-70°F/16-21°C) and humid. At higher levels it is cooler, with less rain, but the air is always moist. Stems bear opposite pairs of lance-shaped leaves. Bright yellow cone of overlapping bracts; white flowers from spring on.

IDEAL CONDITIONS

Temperature In summer 60-65°F/16-18°C. Rest the plant in winter at 55-60°F/16-18°C. Needs a humid atmosphere.
Light Bright, shade from direct sun.
Water Twice a week in summer so the compost is evenly moist, but not waterlogged. In winter every 10 to 14 days to stop compost drying out completely.
Feed Every two weeks from late spring to early autumn.
Pot-on In spring in loam- or peat-based compost.
Propagation Take stem cuttings in spring.

Paphiopedilum callosum
The slipper orchid
comes from subtropical
regions of Nepal and
Assam. Summers are
humid and warm,
70-75°F/21-24°C; winters
much drier, and a little
cooler, 65°F/18°C.
Strap-shaped dark
green leaves are
mottled light green.
Flowers are white,
striped maroon and
green, and have light
purple lips. They
appear in spring.

IDEAL CONDITIONS

Temperature
60-65°F/16-18°C all
year, but in winter,
when building up to
the spring flowering,
drop the temperature
at night to 55-60°F/
13-16°C.
Light A shady
position needed; no
direct sun.
Water Twice a week
in summer to keep
compost moist, not
waterlogged. After
flowering, every 10 to
14 days for 10 weeks,
letting the compost
almost dry out
between waterings.
Feed Monthly, spring
to early autumn.
Pot-on Every two or
three years after it
has flowered, in an
orchid compost.
Propagation Divide
when potting-on.

PROBLEM

Has the plant failed to produce flowers in the
autumn, and are leaf tips turning brown? Is the
air in the room dry?

IF YES

CAUSE Lack of humidity. Foliage will become marked
and plants may refuse to flower in a dry atmosphere.
ACTION Increase humidity around the plant by standing the pot on a tray of wet pebbles or surrounding it
with moist peat. This is most important in very warm
weather, when temperatures are above those recommended in **IDEAL CONDITIONS**.

IF NO

Has the plant been in a constant heat of 60-65°F/
16-18°C during the winter?

IF YES

CAUSE Although this is the ideal daytime range, there
must be a drop in temperature at night in winter if the
plant is to flower well the next season.
CAUSE Ensure that winter night temperatures are
55-60°F/13-16°C; do not leave the plant in a warm,
centrally heated room.

IF NO

Does the foliage also look in a general state of
collapse, with soft, pulpy leaves?

IF YES

CAUSE Overwatering. Unlike many other orchids, this
one does not have pseudobulbs in which it can store
excess water. If the compost is watered too often, it
becomes waterlogged. The roots are starved of
essential oxygen, root rot results, and the plant will
die. The overlapping formation of the leaves creates a
collecting ground for water, which also causes rot if
allowed to remain there during the night in low
temperatures.
ACTION If the plant is in a total state of collapse, let the
compost dry out and watch for signs that the plant
might be reviving. If nothing happens the rot has gone
too far and the plant should be discarded. A plant not
too badly affected should be removed from its pot
and the compost gently teased away from the roots.
Cut away any soft roots and repot in fresh compost
soaked with a fungicide. Thereafter follow watering
instructions as in **IDEAL CONDITIONS**.

PROBLEM

Are the spines losing their brilliant yellow colouring, and has the plant failed to flower?

IF YES

CAUSE Poor light. Plants must have excellent light with direct sun to ensure good spine colour and flowerng. **ACTION** Move the plant to a sunny windowsill where it will get direct sunlight every day.

IF NO

Has the plant been in a heated room in winter?

IF YES

CAUSE It has been denied a winter rest. If the plant is encouraged to grow in winter by keeping it in normal room temperatures, growth in general, and spine colour in particular, will be poor. At this time of year, the level and amount of daylight is not sufficient to sustain continued healthy growth. Flowering the following season may be poor, and plants may not flower at all without a winter rest.
ACTION Nothing immediately, but in late autumn move the plant to a cool room, 48-54°F/9-12°C. It will still require good light with plenty of direct sun.

IF NO

When touched gently, does the globe feel loose in the compost? When you push a finger into the compost does it feel wet just below the surface?

IF YES

CAUSE Overwatering, which has rotted roots—this cactus is particularly sensitive.
ACTION Remove the plant from its pot and gently wash away the compost from the roots. Any dark brown, soft, rotting roots should be cut away. Allow them to dry out for a day or two before repotting in fresh compost. In future follow watering instructions in **IDEAL CONDITIONS**. Should rot be found in winter, withold water completely and repot the plant in spring.

OTHER SPECIES

Parodia sanguiniflora is globular at first, maturing to a cylindrical shape. Groups of white spines with a few brown ones at the centre. Funnel-shaped, bright red flowers in summer.

Parodia chrysacanthion
This cactus is from arid scrub areas of Argentina, with summer temperatures about 70°F/21°C and those in winter 45-50°F/7-10°C. Annual rainfall is around 10in/25cm. The pale green fleshy globes, with yellow spines, store moisture for dry periods. Yellow flowers bloom in late spring and early summer.

IDEAL CONDITIONS

Temperature Normal room temperatures in summer, even in hot weather. Give the cactus a winter rest at 48-54°F/9-12°C.
Light Bright, with direct sun all year.
Water Twice a week in summer, but let surface of compost dry out before watering again. Once a month in winter so compost does not dry out completely.
Feed Monthly, spring to early autumn.
Pot-on In spring in half loam-based compost, half grit.
Propagation Remove offsets. Or sow seed in spring.

Pelargonium × hortorum
Pelargoniums, often called geraniums, are from South Africa. The summers are dry and hot, 65-80°F/18-27°C while winters are wet and cool, 45-50°F/ 7-10°C. The rounded leaves have brownish-red rings. Red, pink and white flowers bloom from spring till autumn.

IDEAL CONDITIONS

Temperature In summer 60°F/16°C, but they will tolerate high temperatures. Rest the plants in winter at 45-50°F/ 7-10°C. Do not expose them to frost.
Light Bright, with direct sun all year.
Water Two or three times a week in summer so that the compost is evenly moist. In the low winter temperatures, water plants once a month to prevent complete drying out.
Feed Every two weeks, late spring to early autumn.
Pot-on In spring in loam- or peat-based compost.
Propagation Take stem cuttings in summer.

PROBLEM

Has the plant grown straggly with small leaves, flowered poorly or not at all?

IF YES

CAUSE Not enough light, if plants are grown in shaded parts of a room, growth will become etiolated and leaves will be small. Flowering also will be poor.
ACTION Move the plant to a windowsill where it will get direct sunlight. Cut down any bare stems to within 6in/15cm of the compost.

IF NO

Has the plant become straggly, producing few flowers, as autumn approaches?

IF YES

CAUSE Natural growth. If the weather is mild, geraniums will last into early winter, but growth will be poor because of the lack of strong daylight.
ACTION Wait until early spring and cut back all the stems to 6in/15cm. When new growth has become established, regularly pinch out growing tips to encourage bushy growth. Early flowers will be lost, but this will ensure many more later on.

PROBLEM

Are the leaves turning yellow and falling, and the flowers and buds dropping? Are there green and black flies on undersides of leaves and flower buds?

IF YES

CAUSE The plant has been attacked by aphids which suck the sap, leaving yellow blotched foliage.
ACTION Badly affected leaves and stems should be removed. Spray with pyrethrum and repeat every few days if insects are still seen.

IF NO

Have the bases of the stems turned black and mushy?

IF YES

CAUSE This is a fungal disease, called blackleg, which is encouraged by overwet conditions. It will also attack cuttings if the compost is kept too wet.
ACTION If all the stems are rotting throw the plant away. Otherwise, remove infected stems, allow the compost to dry out and water as in **IDEAL CONDITIONS**.

PROBLEM

Are the leaf tips turning brown? Are whole leaves turning yellow and falling? Is the air in the room dry?

Pellionia pulchra
Pellionias come from tropical rain forests of S.E. Asia, especially Malaya, where it is hot (75-80°F/24-27°C) and humid, with thundery rain all year. The purple stems bear oval, light green leaves, the veins picked out in purple, with lighter purple on undersides.

IF YES

CAUSE Lack of humidity.
ACTION Create a humid atmosphere: see page 8. Mist spray plants in hanging containers daily.

IF NO

Is the plant near an open door or a door which is opened and closed frequently?

IF YES

CAUSE The plant has been in a draught.
ACTION Move it to a draught-free part of the room.

IF NO

Has the plant been in an unheated room in winter?

IF YES

CAUSE The temperature is too low. Pellionias will tolerate a temperature of 55°F/13°C, but no lower.
ACTION Move the plant to a room with a temperature of 55-65°F/13-18°C; the top heat is better.

IF NO

When you stick a finger into the compost does excess moisture appear on the surface?

IF YES

CAUSE Overwatering, which has rotted the roots.
ACTION If the whole plant is in a state of collapse, throw it away. Otherwise remove the plant from the pot, gently break away the compost from the roots, cut away any brown, soft roots and repot in fresh compost which has been soaked with a fungicide. In future, follow watering instructions as in **IDEAL CONDITIONS**.

IF NO

Are there black flies and tiny white maggots on the surface of the compost?

IF YES

CAUSE The black flies are fungus gnats and the maggots their offspring, which eat decaying foliage.
ACTION Soak the compost with malathion, repeating every few days if the pests persist.

IDEAL CONDITIONS

Temperature The plant can tolerate extreme heat in summer. It can be rested in winter not below 55°F/13°C, but can also remain in a temperature of 65-70°F/18-21°C.
Light Good, but do not expose to direct sunshine.
Water Twice a week in summer so that the compost is always moist. Occasionally in winter to prevent drying out; how often depends on how warm the room is.
Feed Every two weeks, late spring to early autumn.
Pot-on In spring in peat-based compost.
Propagation Take stem cuttings in spring.

Peperomia argyreia
This peperomia is one of many from Central and South America and comes from the tropical rain forests of Brazil. Average temperature is 75-80°F/24-27°C and it rains all year round. The dark green, fleshy leaves marked with silver, are carried on short stems. The plant is semi-succulent and should not be watered too frequently.

IDEAL CONDITIONS

Temperature All year, 60-65°F/ 16-18°C, though it can stand anything down to 50°F/10°C. Needs humidity.
Light Bright with some direct, not scorching sun. Plants with plain green leaves should not have any direct sun.
Water Once every 7 to 10 days in summer; the leaves are semi-succulent and store water. In winter, every two to three weeks.
Feed Monthly, spring to early autumn.
Pot-on Every two or three years in spring in a peat-based compost.
Propagation Stem cuttings in spring and early summer.

PROBLEM

Are the leaf tips turning brown and leaves falling? Is the air in the room dry?

IF YES

CAUSE Insufficient humidity.
CAUSE Create a humid atmosphere around the plant by standing the pot on a tray of wet pebbles or by surrounding it with moist peat. Mist spray in summer, especially in periods of warm weather, but not in winter.

IF NO

Has the plant been in an unheated room in winter?

IF YES

CAUSE The temperature is too low. This plant will tolerate temperatures down to 50°F/10°C, but no lower.
ACTION Move the plant to a room where the temperature is 60-65°F/16-18°C.

IF NO

Are some of the leaves and stems turning black?

IF YES

CAUSE The plant has been overwatered and is starting to rot. The fleshy leaves store a certain amount of water, but they will become saturated and rot will set in if the compost is always kept wet.
ACTION Cut away any badly affected stems and leaves and dust the compost with a fungicide powder. In future, follow the watering instructions given in **IDEAL CONDITIONS**.

PROBLEM

Are the leaves beginning to shrivel? When you push a finger into the compost does it feel dry about 2in/5cm down?

IF YES

CAUSE Underwatering. Although the leaves are semi-succulent and store water, there comes a time when that supply is exhausted and the leaves will start to shrivel.
ACTION Water the compost thoroughly until excess water flows from the hole in the bottom of the pot; let the plant drain before returning it to its saucer.

PROBLEM

Are leaf tips turning brown and papery, and some leaves turning yellow and dying? Does the compost feel dry about 2in/5cm down?

IF YES

CAUSE Underwatering.
ACTION Water the compost, letting excess water drain through the drainage hole in the pot. Thereafter, water as in **IDEAL CONDITIONS**. In the wild, the plant takes up water through its aerial roots as well as through the main root. Indoors the aerial roots can be stuck into the compost in the pot, but in time they crowd out the main roots. It is better to push a moss stick into the pot and grow the philodendron against it, pushing the aerial roots into the moss. Spray the moss daily to keep it moist.

IF NO

When you push a finger into the compost does it feel wet and can moisture be seen on the surface?

IF YES

CAUSE Overwatering. This is most likely to happen in winter when the plant is not in active growth.
ACTION Allow the compost to dry out and in future follow the watering routine in **IDEAL CONDITIONS**. Remove any completely yellow leaves.

IF NO

Has the plant been near a sunny window?

IF YES

CAUSE The leaves have been scorched. This can easily happen if there is any water on the leaves.
ACTION Move the plant to a spot in which it will have bright light, but no direct sun.

PROBLEM

Are the leaves looking dull and losing their coppery sheen? Is the foliage straggly and sparse?

IF YES

CAUSE Not enough light.
ACTION Move the plant closer to a window to get bright light, but no direct sun. Cut any bare stems to within 6in/15cm of the compost; make the cut just above the point where a leaf joins the main stem. The plant can also be pruned back in this manner.

Philodendron erubescens
Philodendron is a climber native to Colombian tropical rain forests; it clings to tree trunks and branches by means of aerial roots. Temperature all year is 75-80°F/24-27°C, the air is moist, and rain falls regularly. The plant's arrowhead leaves open pink but turn dark coppery green, with red undersides.

IDEAL CONDITIONS

Temperature In summer, 65-75°F/18-24°C. Rest the plant in winter at 60-65°F/16-18°C, with a minimum of 55°F/13°C.
Light Bright, to keep good leaf colour, but not direct sunlight.
Water Twice a week in summer so compost is always moist. Once a week in winter to avoid drying out.
Pot-on In spring in peat-based compost. In time the plant will grow too large to be potted-on. Instead, each year in spring, replace the top 2in/5cm or so of compost with fresh.
Propagation Take cuttings in spring.

P H O E N I X

Phoenix canariensis
The date palm is native to the Canary Islands, where summers are dry and warm, 60-70°F/16-21°C, and winters mild, 50-55°F/10-13°C. The palm grows only a few inches a year, but the fronds spread quite widely. Each frond is erect at the base, then arches, with tapering pinnae.

IDEAL CONDITIONS

Temperature In summer, 65-70°F/18-21°C. If possible, put the plant outdoors in summer in a sheltered spot. Give a winter rest at 55-60°F/13-16°C.
Light Bright, with direct sun all year; most important in short daylight hours of winter.
Water Two or three times a week in summer so compost is evenly moist. In winter, every 7 to 10 days to keep compost just moist.
Feed Every two weeks, late spring to early autumn.
Pot-on In spring in loam-based compost.
Propagation Sow seeds in spring, but germination is slow.

PROBLEM

Are the tips of the leaflets browning? Have whole fronds turned brown and dry? Does the compost feel dry about 2in/5cm down?

=== IF YES ===

CAUSE Underwatering.
ACTION Thoroughly water the compost until water comes out of the drainage hole in the pot. Then follow the watering instructions in **IDEAL CONDITIONS**.

=== IF NO ===

Are the fronds turning brown in winter?

=== IF YES ===

CAUSE The palm has been too warm. This is likely to happen if it is overwintered in the warm dry air of centrally heated rooms.
ACTION Keep the plant at 55-60°F/13-16°C in winter.

=== IF NO ===

Have newly emerging fronds turned brown?

=== IF YES ===

CAUSE Scorching by the sun. While the palm needs sun, young tender fronds are harmed by very hot sun.
ACTION During the time the fronds are emerging, move the palm out of the line of direct sun or shade it with a translucent blind or curtain.

=== IF NO ===

Is the compost wet and slimy just below the surface?

=== IF YES ===

CAUSE Overwatering, which can rot the roots.
ACTION If the whole plant is in a state of collapse, throw it away; it is too far gone to be rescued. Otherwise allow the compost to dry out, then follow the watering instructions **IDEAL CONDITIONS**.

=== PROBLEM ===

Are the lower leaves turning yellow? Has the plant been in a shady part of the room?

=== IF YES ===

CAUSE Insufficient light.
ACTION Move the plant closer to a bright window where it will get direct sunlight; this is particularly important during the short daylight hours of winter.

Pilea cadieri

PROBLEM

Are the edges of the leaves brown or are whole leaves turning brown and falling? Is the plant in constantly dry heat at about 65°F/18°C?

━━━━━━━━ IF YES ━━━━━━━━

CAUSE Lack of humidity.
ACTION Mist spray the plant daily. To increase humidity in the long term, see page 8.

━━━━━━━━ IF NO ━━━━━━━━

Are there fine white webs on the leaves and stems?

━━━━━━━━ IF YES ━━━━━━━━

CAUSE A sign of the presence of red spider mites, attracted by dry warm conditions. They suck the sap, discolouring the foliage and leaving yellow spots.
ACTION Wipe away all traces of the webs and spray the plant with liquid derris. Repeat every few days while the mites persist. Increase the level of humidity.

━━━━━━━━ IF NO ━━━━━━━━

Has the plant been in an unheated room in winter?

━━━━━━━━ IF YES ━━━━━━━━

CAUSE The temperature has been too low. While the plant will survive at 50°F/10°C for a short time, it is unwise to keep it at that level for long.
ACTION Move the plant to a room with a temperature of 55-65°F/13-18°C. Remove any badly marked leaves.

━━━━━━━━ IF NO ━━━━━━━━

Do stems look brown and mushy at compost level?

━━━━━━━━ IF YES ━━━━━━━━

CAUSE Stem rot disease, brought on by overwatering.
ACTION If all stems are rotten, throw the plant away. If only a few, cut them out completely, dust the compost with fungicide powder and let it dry out. Thereafter, water as in **IDEAL CONDITIONS**.

━━━━━━━ **PROBLEM** ━━━━━━━

Is the plant leggy, with large gaps between leaves?

━━━━━━━━ IF YES ━━━━━━━━

CAUSE Natural; this happens after about 18 months.
ACTION In spring, cut down the stems to 4in/10cm. When new growth is established, pinch out growing tips regularly to encourage bushy growth.

Pileas are tropical plants, this one from Vietnam's rain forests. Temperatures average 75-80°F/24-27°C, the air is always humid, and there is rain all year. The stems of the plant, which creep along the ground, bear oval, quilted dark green leaves, marked with silver.

IDEAL CONDITIONS

Temperature 55-65°F/13-18°C all year, but it tolerates a temperature down to 50°F/10°C. It should have humidity.
Light Bright, but not in direct sunlight. It will even grow in slight shade.
Water Two or three times a week in summer, so the compost is constantly moist. In winter once a week, so compost does not dry out completely.
Feed Every two weeks from late spring to early autumn.
Pot-on In spring in loam- or peat-based compost.
Propagation Take cuttings in spring or summer.

**P
L
A
T
Y
C
E
R
I
U
M**

Platycerium bifurcatum
The staghorn fern is an unusual-looking epiphyte which grows on trees in rain forests of Australia and the East Indies. The climate is hot, 75-80°F/24-27°C, the air always humid. Bright green fronds, forked like a stag's horns, emerge from the centre of sterile circular fronds.

IDEAL CONDITIONS

Temperature In summer, 60-70°F/16-21°C. Rest the fern in winter at 60-65°F/16-18°C. Needs a humid atmosphere.
Light Bright, but no direct sunlight.
Water About once a week in summer allowing the compost almost to dry out between waterings. In winter, every 10 days, so compost is barely moist.
Feed Monthly, from spring to early autumn.
Pot-on Every three years in spring in half peat and half sphagnum moss.
Propagation From spores on the undersides of the fronds.

PROBLEM

Are the fronds becoming pale, with disfiguring marks over the surface and along the edges?

=== IF YES ===

CAUSE The fern has been exposed to direct sunlight.
ACTION Move it to a place out of the direct line of the sun but where it will get a bright light.

=== IF NO ===

Is the atmosphere in the room warm and dry?

=== IF YES ===

CAUSE Lack of humidity.
ACTION Increase humidity: see page 8. This fern is often grown in a hanging container; if so, mist spray it every second day. More frequent spraying may remove the waxy coating on the fronds.

=== IF NO ===

Do the fronds also appear to be limp?

=== IF YES ===

CAUSE Underwatering. The compost should almost dry out between waterings, but not completely.
ACTION Thoroughly water the plant. This is best done by immersing the pot in water to within 2in/5cm of the rim. Leave it to soak for about 15 minutes, then let any excess water drain away.

=== IF NO ===

Are the undersides of the fronds covered with soft, light brown or hard, dark brown bumps?

=== IF YES ===

CAUSE These are scale insects, which suck the sap, leaving yellow spots that later turn brown.
ACTION If there are only a few, scrape them off with a fingernail. If many, spray with dimethoate. Inspect the fronds regularly for any sign of these insects.

=== PROBLEM ===

Are the circular fronds that surround the forked fronds turning brown and dying off?

=== IF YES ===

CAUSE This is natural; they will soon be replaced.
ACTION Remove any completely dry and dead fronds.

PROBLEM

Is growth weak and spindly, and has the plant failed to flower or flowered poorly?

=========================== IF YES ===========================

CAUSE The plant has been denied a winter rest.
ACTION None for the moment, but in late autumn move the plant to a room with a temperature between 45-50°F/7-10°C. It will also require good light with all the sun it can get at this time of the year. In spring, cut back all the stems by two-thirds. If the plant is not pruned, it may flower poorly or not at all since the flowers are produced only on new growth.

=========================== IF NO ===========================

Has the plant produced a few flowers but failed to flower continuously throughout the summer?

=========================== IF YES ===========================

CAUSE Not enough light and, in particular, not enough direct sunshine.
ACTION Move the plant close to a window where it will get several hours of sunlight every day.

=========================== IF NO ===========================

Are the roots showing through the drainage hole in the bottom of the pot?

=========================== IF YES ===========================

CAUSE The plant requires potting-on. The roots have filled the pot, displacing the compost which holds the moisture and food vital for healthy, vigorous growth.
ACTION If the pot is completely filled with roots, pot-on to a container 2in/5cm larger in diameter. The compost will provide nutrients for the plant for about three months, but the plant should then be fed as in **IDEAL CONDITIONS**.

=========================== IF NO ===========================

Is the plant generally getting out of hand, with long sprawling stems?

=========================== IF YES ===========================

CAUSE This is plumbago's natural growth pattern.
ACTION Train the stems around a wire hoop, with the two ends pushed into the compost, or against a small plastic trellis. One or two stems could be cut back, but you run the risk of having far fewer flowers in future.

Plumbago capensis
Plumbago is a flowering climber from Cape Province, South Africa. The climate is subtropical: dry summers 65°F/18°C; damp winters 55°F/13°C. In northern hemisphere, keep the plant moist in summer, fairly dry in winter. Long stems with oval green leaves and clusters of pale blue flowers, from spring.

IDEAL CONDITIONS

Temperature In summer, 50-55°F/ 10-13°C, but the plant will stand much warmer weather. A rest period in winter at about 50°F/10°C is needed; the minimum is 45°F/7°C.
Light Bright, direct sunlight especially on short winter days.
Water Twice a week in summer to keep compost moist, not sodden. In winter, every 10 to 14 days to prevent drying out.
Feed Every two weeks from late spring to early autumn.
Pot-on In early spring in loam-based compost.
Propagation Take stem cuttings in early summer.

Pteris cretica
'Albolineata'
The pteris fern is found
in tropical rain forests in
many parts of the world.
It needs high humidity,
plenty of rain, and
warmth (75°F/24°C).
Roots must always be
well watered. Stems
have four bright green,
strap-shaped leaflets,
each with a whitish
green stripe along its
entire length.

IDEAL CONDITIONS

Temperature In
summer, 60-65°F/
16-18°C, but the fern
tolerates higher
temperatures as long
as humidity, too, is
high. In winter, rest
the plant at
55-60°F/13-16°C.
Light Bright, out of
direct sunlight.
Water Two or three
times a week to keep
compost moist. Once
or twice a week in
winter.
Feed Every two
weeks from late
spring to early
autumn.
Pot-on In spring in
equal parts of loam,
peat and sand, for
good drainage, or in
peat-based compost.
Propagation Divide
in spring. Or sow
spores.

PROBLEM

Are the fronds shrivelling and dying? When you
push a finger into the compost does it feel dry
about 2in/5cm below the surface?

IF YES

CAUSE The plant has been allowed to dry out. The
roots of pteris ferns need to be moist at all times of the
year, even when they are resting. But remember that
plants kept in lower temperatures require less frequent watering than those in a centrally heated room.
ACTION If the plant has been dry for any length of time,
the roots may well have been killed and the plant will
have to be discarded, but first try to revive it. Cut
away all the dead fronds at compost level and
thoroughly water the compost until excess water
drains from the pot. If the compost has shrunk from the
sides of the pot, immerse it in a bowl of water to within
2in/5cm of the pot rim. Leave until moisture is seen on
the compost surface. Spray the stubble daily, and if
the roots have not been affected new growth should
soon appear. In future, follow watering instructions as
in **IDEAL CONDITIONS**.

PROBLEM

Are the fronds turning brown at the tips? Has the plant
been in a warm centrally heated room?

IF YES

CAUSE Insufficient humidity. Dry air does not seem to
bother this plant below 65°F/18°C, but if the
temperature is much above that humidity becomes
important.
ACTION Increase humidity around the plant: see page
8. A daily mist spray also helps.

IF NO

Has the plant been near a sunny window?

IF YES

CAUSE Sun has scorched the leaves.
ACTION Move the plant to a position where it will have
bright light but no direct sun. Variegated forms must
always have bright light to maintain the leaf colour.

OTHER SPECIES

Pteris ensiformis 'Victoriae' has darker green
fronds with silvery markings along the ribs.

PROBLEM

Has the plant failed to flower? Has it spent the winter in a warm, centrally heated room?

IF YES

CAUSE The plant has not had a winter rest at a low temperature, which is vital for successful flowering.
ACTION None for the moment, but in late autumn move the plant to an unheated room, at 45°F/7°C, with good light. Plants should not be exposed to frost.

IF NO

Has the plant been in a shaded part of the room?

IF YES

CAUSE Not enough light. This cactus must have bright light with sun all year round.
ACTION Move the plant to a windowsill where it will get direct sun. It may not flower this year, but continued good light followed by a winter rest, again in good light, should ensure flowering next season.

IF NO

Are there white woolly patches on the stems?

IF YES

CAUSE The plant has been attacked by mealy bugs, often difficult to detect because the clumps of globular stems are packed closely. These insects cocoon themselves in a white waxy coating.
ACTION Gently brush away the woolly patches, taking care not to damage the short spines. Spray with liquid derris and repeat every few days if the insects persist. If root mealy bugs are found, the compost should be drenched with dimethoate.

PROBLEM

Are the bases of the globes turning brown, and do they feel soft and mushy?

IF YES

CAUSE The stems are rotting through overwatering.
ACTION If the rot has not gone too far, the plant may be saved by cutting away badly rotted globes, dusting the compost surface with a fungicide powder, and allowing the compost to dry out. Thereafter, follow watering instructions as in **IDEAL CONDITIONS**. If all the globes are rotting, throw the plant away.

Rebutia miniscula
Rebutia is a cactus from scrub areas of Argentina. In summer, temperatures may reach 100°F/38°C and rain falls only in short downpours. Winters are cold and fairly dry, but the clumps of globe-shaped stems conserve water. Many red trumpet-shaped flowers appear in late spring and summer, even on quite young plants.

IDEAL CONDITIONS

Temperature Normal room temperatures in summer, but needs a well-ventilated position. Essential to rest the cactus in winter around 45°F/7°C.
Light Bright with direct sun all year.
Water Twice a week in summer, but let surface of compost dry out between waterings. In winter, once a week.
Feed Every two weeks from late spring to early autumn.
Pot-on In spring in two parts loam compost to one part sand. Good drainage is essential.
Propagation Divide in summer. Sow seed in spring.

Rhipsalidopsis gaertneri
The Easter cactus is an epiphyte found on trees in rain forests of Brazil. Average temperature is 75°F/24°C, and the air is always humid. Flattened stems have jointed segments and areoles on stem edges bear bristles and brick-red flowers in spring. With its arching stems, this plant looks good in a hanging basket.

IDEAL CONDITIONS

Temperature In summer, 65-75°F/18-24°C. Rest the cactus at 55°F/13°C in winter; below 50°F/10°C will kill it.
Light Always bright, but not direct sun.
Water In summer, twice a week and spray often. If the cactus is in a cool room in winter, water about every two weeks; more often in a heated room.
Feed Every three weeks after flower buds show until early autumn.
Pot-on In two parts loam-based compost to one part sand after flowering.
Propagation Take stem cuttings of two or three segments in summer.

PROBLEM

Has the plant failed to flower or flowered poorly? Is it in a dark corner of the room?

IF YES

CAUSE Not enough light. This cactus must have good light if it is to flower well.
ACTION Move the plant closer to a window, but do not expose it to direct sun. If possible, put the plant outside in summer in a sheltered, shady spot. It may not flower this year, but you should have better luck next season.

IF NO

Has the plant been in a constant winter temperature of 70°F/21°C or more?

IF YES

CAUSE It has not had a winter rest period. This cactus will thrive in warmth all year but lower temperatures in winter usually ensure prolific flowering.
ACTION Nothing immediately, but in late autumn put the plant in a room in which the temperature is around 55°F/13°C. Below 50°F/10°C, the plant will be harmed. When flower buds first show, bring the plant into a temperature of 65-75°F/18-24°C.

PROBLEM

Are the stems breaking off at compost level? Do they feel soft and mushy at this point?

IF YES

CAUSE Overwatering, which has encouraged rotting.
ACTION Remove all the stems that feel soft at the base. Dust the compost with a fungicide powder and let it dry out. In future, follow watering instructions in **IDEAL CONDITIONS**.

PROBLEM

Are the stems shrivelling?

IF YES

CAUSE Underwatering. The fleshy stems store a certain amount of water, but when this has been used up and the compost is dry they begin to shrivel.
ACTION Water the compost until excess water drains from the bottom of the pot. In future, do not allow the compost to dry out.

PROBLEM

Are the flower buds, open flowers and leaves falling rapidly? Is the plant in a warm centrally heated room?

IF YES

CAUSE The temperature is too high. Any length of time in a warm room will almost always kill the plant.
ACTION Move it to an unheated room or one where the heat is very restricted, ideally 45-55°F/7-13°C.

IF NO

Is the atmosphere in the room dry?

IF YES

CAUSE Lack of humidity, which is important all year round, not only when the plant is in flower.
ACTION Increase the humidity: see page 8. A daily overhead mist spray will also help.

IF NO

When you push a finger into the compost does it feel dry about 2in/5cm below the surface?

IF YES

CAUSE Not enough water.
ACTION Water the compost until excess water drains from the bottom of the pot. In future, follow watering instructions in **IDEAL CONDITIONS**. If the compost has shrunk from the pot sides, immerse the pot in a pail of water to within 2in/5cm of the rim. Leave for about 30 minutes until the compost is moist.

PROBLEM

Are the leaves turning yellow?

IF YES

CAUSE Watering with hard water, which contains lime. Azaleas are lime-hating plants.
ACTION Always water with soft water or rainwater.

PROBLEM

Is the plant losing its symmetrical shape?

IF YES

CAUSE Natural growth of the plant.
ACTION Trim any overlong stems to retain shape. Always remove dead flower heads and seed pods, or the plant will produce seeds instead of flowers.

Rhododendron simsii **Indian azaleas** originated in temperate forests of China, with temperatures up to 75°F/24°C in summer and down to 45°F/7°C in winter. Rain falls all year. The oval dark green leaves are leathery; red, purple and white flowers bloom in spring, unless forced for Christmas. It is not able to stand hot rooms.

IDEAL CONDITIONS

Temperature In summer 65°F/18°C; if much warmer more humidity will be needed. Winter at 45-55°F/7-13°C; the lower, the better.
Light Bright, shade from direct sun. Put plant outdoors in summer in a shady, sheltered spot.
Water Twice a week in summer to keep compost evenly moist. Every 10 to 14 days in winter. Use soft water.
Feed Every two weeks late spring to early autumn with an acid fertilizer.
Pot-on After flowering in peat-based compost.
Propagation Take stem cuttings in summer.

RHODODENDRON

Rhoeo spathacea
Rhoeo is native to high rain forest areas of the West Indies and Mexico. Temperatures average 70°F/21°C and rain falls evenly during the year. Lance-shaped leaves grow as a rosette, forming a stem as they die; they are green on top, purple below. Purple boat-shaped bracts and white flowers appear from late spring.

IDEAL CONDITIONS

Temperature In summer, around 60°F/16°C, but the plant adjusts to higher temperatures. Rest it in winter at 50°F/10°C, and never lower. Needs a humid atmosphere.
Light Bright, with no direct sun.
Water Two or three times a week in summer, so compost is evenly moist. Once a week in winter. Allow surface to dry out between waterings.
Feed Every two weeks from late spring to early autumn.
Pot-on Every other year in loam- or peat-based compost.
Propagated From off-sets when potting-on.

PROBLEM

Are the edges of the leaves turning brown? Is the plant in a warm dry room?

IF YES

CAUSE Lack of humidity.
ACTION Create humidity: see page 8. A daily overhead mist spray will also be beneficial.

IF NO

Has the plant been in an unheated room in winter?

IF YES

CAUSE The temperature is too low. Rhoeos will not tolerate temperatures below 50°F/10°C.
ACTION Move the plant to a room at about 55°F/13°C; a little higher is advisable if the plant is in a bad state.

IF NO

Has the plant been in the sun, especially in summer?

IF YES

CAUSE The leaves have been scorched. They will scorch extremely easily if they are mist sprayed and then exposed to direct sun.
ACTION Move the plant to a part of the room where it will have good light but not be in direct sunlight. Any badly disfigured leaves should be removed.

PROBLEM

Has the plant failed to produce the colourful bracts and flowers? Are the leaves paling? Is it in a shaded part of the room?

IF YES

CAUSE Insufficient light.
ACTION Move the plant closer to a window where it will get good light without direct sun.

PROBLEM

Does the central stem feel soft and mushy at the level of the compost? Has the plant collapsed?

IF YES

CAUSE The stem is rotting through overwatering.
ACTION None at this stage; you must resign yourself to the loss of the plant. Replace it and follow watering instructions in **IDEAL CONDITIONS**.

PROBLEM

Are the leaves wilting, turning brown, curling and falling? When you push a finger into the compost does it feel dry about 2in/5cm down?

IF YES

CAUSE Underwatering. At first the leaves wilt and if they are left without water for any length of time they begin to brown and fall.
ACTION Remove any badly browned leaves. Water the compost thoroughly. If the compost has shrunk from the side of the pot immerse it in a pail of water to within 2in/5cm of the pot rim. Leave for about 30 minutes and allow any excess water to drain away.

IF NO

Has the plant been exposed to direct sunlight?

IF YES

CAUSE The leaves have been scorched. If leaves are wet and exposed to direct sun, the scorching will be even more widespread.
ACTION Move the plant away from the window to a position with good light but no direct sun.

IF NO

Is the plant in a dry centrally heated room in winter?

IF YES

CAUSE Lack of humidity.
ACTION Increase humidity by spraying the plant daily. For a longer-term effect see page 8.

IF NO

Are the leaves of the plant touching a wall?

IF YES

CAUSE Wall plaster, which is absorbent, is drawing moisture out of the leaves, so they are going brown.
ACTION Move the plant away from the wall.

PROBLEM

Is the plant getting out of hand and growing too tall?

IF YES

CAUSE Natural growth, but it can be kept in check.
ACTION Cut back stems in late spring or early summer to the desired height. When new growth appears, pinch out growing tips to promote bushy browth.

Rhoicissus capensis
Rhoicissus is an evergreen climber from bush areas of the Cape Province, South Africa. Warm summers, 70°F/21°C or much higher. Winters mild, 50-55°F/10-13°C. Rain all year, but winter wetter than summer. Heart-shaped glossy bright green leaves, serrated edges. Stakes needed for tendrils to cling to.

IDEAL CONDITIONS

Temperature In summer, 55-65°F/13-18°C. Rest the plant in winter at about 50°F/10°C. It will tolerate higher temperatures but winter growth may be weak.
Light Bright, but no direct sunlight.
Water Twice a week in summer so that compost stays evenly moist. Every 10 to 14 days in winter if the plant is in the cool; in a warm room it will have to be watered more often.
Feed Every two weeks, late spring to early autumn.
Pot-on In spring in a loam-based compost.
Propagation Take stem cuttings in summer.

Saintpaulia ionantha
African violets are
found in tropical rain
forests of East Africa.
Average temperature is
70-80°F/21-27°C, with
rain all year. Leaves are
heart-shaped and
velvety, and the many
cultivars bear single or
double white, pink, red,
blue or purple flowers.
With good light, plants
bloom year round.

IDEAL CONDITIONS

Temperature All
year at 60-70°F/
16-21°C; lower
temperatures will kill
the plant. Also needs
a humid atmosphere.
Light Bright, but not
direct sunlight.
Water Twice a week
throughout the year.
Never water directly
on to the leaves. It is
safer to immerse the
pot in 2in/5cm of
water for 30 minutes.
If watering from
above, pour water
around the side of the
pot, not on the crown
of the plant.
Feed Monthly, spring
to early autumn.
Pot-on Every two or
three years in spring
in peat-based
compost.
Propagation Leaf
cuttings in spring.

PROBLEM

Are the leaves wilting and curling at the edges?
Is the plant in a warm, centrally heated room
with a dry atmosphere?

IF YES

CAUSE Lack of humidity.
ACTION Increase humidity: see page 8. Do not mist
spray leaves; this will mark them for good.

IF NO

Do the stems look floppy and do they feel soft where
they emerge from the compost? When you push a
finger into the compost does it feel wet?

IF YES

CAUSE The plant has been overwatered, resulting in
stem rot disease.
ACTION If only a few stems are affected, remove them
completely, dust the compost with a fungicide
powder and allow the compost to dry out. Thereafter,
follow watering instructions in **IDEAL CONDITIONS**. If all
the stems are rotten, and the short scaly trunk that
develops on mature plants is also soft and mushy, the
crown has rotted. There is nothing that can be done;
throw the plant away before it infects any others.

IF NO

Is there also yellow mottling on the leaves? Has
growth become distorted and stunted?

IF YES

CAUSE An attack of virus disease, which is spread by
insects from plant to plant.
ACTION Unfortunately, there is no cure and the plant
should be discarded immediately. Throw away the
compost as well, since this harbours the virus. Pots
should be washed out and sterilized.

PROBLEM

Has the plant flowered poorly or not at all? Is it in a
shaded part of the room?

IF YES

CAUSE Not enough light. For successful flowering, it
must have bright light; this is especially important in
the short hours of winter daylight.
ACTION Move the plant to a windowsill where it will
have bright light, but no direct sun.

PROBLEM

Does the plant appear to have stopped growing; are the leaves turning pale and losing their bright markings? Is the plant in a dark corner?

IF YES

CAUSE Insufficient light. A sansevieria will not object to a slightly shaded spot, but deep gloom will bring growth to a virtual standstill and affect leaf colour.
ACTION Move the plant closer to a window where it will have direct sun. Acclimatize plants to more intense light slowly by moving them a little closer to the window every day. Sudden exposure to strong light is likely to burn the leaves.

IF NO

Do the leaf tips show signs of damage?

IF YES

CAUSE Usually careless handling of the plant when leaves are cleaned or knocking against it. Once the tip is damaged, the leaf will grow no more for the tip is its growth point.
ACTION Nothing can be done, but in future take care when cleaning leaves and repot large, top-heavy plants from plastic pots into more stable clay pots.

PROBLEM

Are there soft brown patches on the leaves? When you push a finger into the compost does it feel wet just below the surface?

IF YES

CAUSE Overwatering. The fleshy leaves store water to draw on in dry periods, but if the compost is always wet and leaves have reached saturation point, soft discoloured patches will result.
ACTION Allow the compost to dry out. Any permanently damaged leaves should be removed completely. In future water as in **IDEAL CONDITIONS**.

IF NO

Do the leaves also look mushy at compost level?

IF YES

CAUSE Overwatering, resulting in stem rot disease.
ACTION None if all are rotting. Throw the plant away. In mild infections, cut away the rotten leaves, dust compost with a fungicide powder.

Sansevieria trifasciata 'Laurentii'
Sansevieria is a succulent native to grassland areas of S. Africa. Summers are 65-80°F/18-27°C, winters 55°F/13°C, with most rain in summer. The fleshy leaves store water against the dry winter. The mid-green, sword-shaped leaves, with darker horizontal bands and yellow edges, grow from an underground rhizome.

IDEAL CONDITIONS

Temperature All year 65-75°F/18-24°C. In winter 55°F/13°C is tolerated, but growth stops. 60°F/16°C or above is far better.
Light Bright, with direct sun all year, though some shade is acceptable.
Water Once a week in summer, once a month in winter.
Feed Monthly, spring to early autumn.
Pot-on Every two or three years in spring, in two parts loam-based compost to one part sand.
Propagation Remove offsets when potting-on. Or take leaf cuttings in summer, but the new plants will be plain green.

Saxifraga stolonifera
Mother of thousands
comes from the
temperate forests of
China, with warm
summers (75°F/24°C)
and cool winters to
45°F/7°C. Rain falls all
year round. Slightly
hairy dark green leaves
have silvery veins and
red undersides; starry
flowers bloom in
summer. It spreads by
producing replicas of
itself at the tips of
runners.

IDEAL CONDITIONS

Temperature In
summer, 50-60°F/
10-16°C is best. It will
tolerate a higher
temperature but
greater humidity is
then needed. In
winter, rest the plant
at 45-50°F/7-10°C.
Light Bright with an
hour or two of direct
sun each day, but not
when it is fierce.
Water Two or three
times a week in
summer so compost
is always moist. Once
a week in winter.
Feed Monthly, spring
to early autumn.
Pot-on In spring in
loam-based compost.
Propagation Remove
plantlets in summer
and pot-up or layer
the runners in a pot
of compost.

PROBLEM

Are leaf stalks becoming lanky, and is growth
generally weak and floppy? Is the plant in a
shaded part of the room away from the window?

IF YES

CAUSE Not enough light. Growth will be poor with few
runners produced in these conditions.
ACTION Move the plant closer to a window where it will
have bright light with some direct sun. Shade from
fierce midday sun. These plants look best hanging in
a container in front of a window.

IF NO

Are the leaves also paling and losing their silvery
markings on the veins?

IF YES

CAUSE Again, not enough light.
ACTION Move the plant to a lighter spot in the room.

IF NO

Has the plant been in a warm room in winter?

IF YES

CAUSE Too much heat. The combination of high winter
temperatures and inadequate daylight results in
poor, lanky growth.
ACTION Move the plant to a room with a temperature of
45-50°F/7-10°C.

IF NO

Have there been periods of very warm weather
during the summer?

IF YES

CAUSE The air too dry.
ACTION Increase humidity: see page 8. Plants in
hanging containers should be sprayed daily.

IF NO

Is the foliage generally sparse and are few new
runners being produced?

IF YES

CAUSE Old age. The plant is nearing the end of its
useful life.
ACTION Now is the time to propagate from the plantlets
on the ends of the runners as in **IDEAL CONDITIONS**.

PROBLEM

Are there brown patches on the leaves, and are leaf edges turning brown? Is the plant in a warm, dry centrally heated room?

IF YES

CAUSE Lack of humidity. If the temperature is under 65°F/18°C, leaves should not be affected; but if it is higher and the air is dry, leaves will be damaged.
ACTION Create a humid atmosphere: see page 8. Mist spray the leaves regularly.

IF NO

Has the plant been exposed to direct sun?

IF YES

CAUSE The leaves have been scorched. If sunlight falls on wet leaves, they are likely to be scorched.
ACTION Move the plant out of the direct line of the sun to a position in which it will still get bright light.

IF NO

Are the leaves and stems also covered with white powder and fine white webs?

IF YES

CAUSE The plant has been infested with red spider mites, encouraged by a warm, dry atmosphere.
ACTION Spray with liquid derris. Should the pests persist, spray again a few days later. Maintain a humid atmosphere to keep them at bay.

PROBLEM

Are the leaflets falling? Has the plant been in an unheated room in winter?

IF YES

CAUSE It has been too cold. The minimum winter temperature for this plant is 55°F/13°C.
ACTION Move the plant to a room with a temperature around 60°F/16°C.

PROBLEM

Are the leaves losing their bright colour?

IF YES

CAUSE The plant is not being fed regularly.
ACTION Apply a regular liquid feed to the compost every two weeks, late spring to early autumn.

Schefflera actinophylla
The umbrella plant is at home in tropical rain forests of Queensland, Australia, where it is hot (75-85°F/24-30°C) and humid. Rain is heaviest in late summer and early autumn. The central stem bears stalks with six or more bright green, glossy, oval leaflets rather like an open umbrella in shape.

IDEAL CONDITIONS

Temperature In summer, 60-65°F/16-18°C. Rest the plant in winter at 55-60°F/13-16°C; the nearer to 60°F/16°C the better.
Light Bright, but keep it out of direct sun. It will grow in a slightly shady spot.
Water Twice a week in summer so the compost is evenly moist. Once a week in winter to prevent the compost drying out completely.
Feed Every two weeks, late spring to early autumn.
Pot-on In spring in a loam-based compost.
Propagation By sowing fresh seed in spring. Bottom heat is needed for germination.

Schlumbergera truncata
Schlumbergera is an epiphytic cactus from the hot, humid rain forests of southern Brazil. It is also sold as *Zygocactus truncatus*, or crab or claw cactus. The mid-green stems are flat, jointed segments with toothed edges. Red, pendant flowers with tiers of turned-back petals appear in winter at the tops of the stems.

IDEAL CONDITIONS

Temperature In summer, 65-75°F/18-24°C. Rest plants briefly, early autumn to early winter, at 55-60°F/13-16°C.
Light Bright, but no direct sun.
Water Frequently in the growth period to keep compost always moist. From early autumn, water only occasionally. Increase when buds form, and give less for a few weeks after flowering.
Feed Every three weeks except just after flowering.
Pot-on In spring in two parts loam-based compost to one part sand.
Propagation By stem cuttings of 2-3 segments in summer.

PROBLEM

Have the flower buds started to drop off the plant before they have opened?

IF YES

CAUSE Schlumbergera is susceptible to leaf drop, a common cause being that the plant has been moved after the buds have begun to form. The buds then turn to the direction from which the light is now coming, are damaged in doing so and later drop off.
ACTION Once the buds have fallen nothing can be done to make the cactus flower again this year. Next autumn, move the plant at the end of its rest period to the position in which it is to flower before the buds form, and do not turn it around.

IF NO

Is the compost wet just below the surface?

IF YES

CAUSE The roots are waterlogged. This plant is a native of rain forests but because it grows on tree branches, the roots never stand in water.
ACTION Let the compost dry out considerably to avoid further damage to the plant, thereafter water as in **IDEAL CONDITIONS**. Use a well-draining compost.

IF NO

When you push in a finger, is the compost dry 2in/5cm down?

IF YES

CAUSE The roots are far too dry.
ACTION Water thoroughly, then follow instructions in **IDEAL CONDITIONS**. The compost must never dry out.

PROBLEM

Are there no signs of the cactus producing buds?

IF YES

CAUSE The cactus has had too much light when the buds should have been forming; it needs limited daylight during the rest period to promote budding.
ACTION In early autumn, put the cactus in a slightly cooler room where it will be in darkness overnight. Take it back into warmth and unlimited light at the first sign of budding to prevent leaf drop. Try to place it so that the light still falls from the same direction.

Scindapsus aureus
Devil's ivy is found in tropical rain forests of the Solomon Islands in the Pacific. Always hot, 75-80°F/24-27°C average, and humid, with rain all year, but heaviest in summer and autumn. The climber's long stems carry green leaves splashed with yellow, which open oval, then become heart-shaped.

◀ PROBLEM ▶

Are there brown marks on the leaves, and are the edges turning brown? Are they shrivelling? Is the compost dry about 2in/5cm down?

IF YES

CAUSE Underwatering. The surface of the compost should be allowed to dry out between waterings, but if the compost deeper down dries out completely the roots may be permanently damaged. Check the compost for moisture regularly by pushing a finger a little way into it.
ACTION Thoroughly water the compost until any excess runs out of the drainage hole in the pot. If the compost has shrunk from the side of the pot, immerse it in a pail of water to within 2in/5cm of the pot's rim. Leave for about 30 minutes until the compost is soaked, and allow excess water to drain away before returning the pot to its saucer.

IF NO

Is the plant in a dry, centrally heated room in the winter?

IF YES

CAUSE The air is too dry. Plants kept in lower temperatures during the winter do not need a humid atmosphere.
ACTION Increase humidity around the plant by standing the pot on a tray of wet pebbles or surrounding it with moist peat. Regular mist spraying will also help.

IF NO

Has the plant been in an unheated room in winter?

IF YES

CAUSE Insufficient warmth. The minimum acceptable winter temperature is 55°F/13°C.
ACTION Move the plant to a room with a temperature around 60°F/16°C.

PROBLEM

Are the leaves reverting to plain green?

IF YES

CAUSE Not enough light. Variegated plants must have good light or they will revert to green.
ACTION Move the plant to a position in which it will get bright light but not direct sunlight.

IDEAL CONDITIONS

Temperature In summer, 65-70°F/18-21°C. Give the plant a winter rest around 60°F/16°C and never below 55°F/13°C.
Light Bright, but no scorching sun. Sunlight filtered through a translucent curtain or blind is acceptable.
Water Twice a week in summer but let surface dry out before watering again. Once a week in winter, so compost is not completely dry.
Feed Every two weeks, late spring to early autumn.
Pot-on Every other year in peat-based compost.
Propagation Take stem cuttings in summer.

S E D U M

Sedum morganianum
This sedum is a succulent native to the high, dry scrublands of Mexico, with summer temperature 60-75°F/16-24°C, winter 45-50°F/7-10°C; most rain falls in summer. The leaves are able to store water to use in dry periods. The fleshy, tail-like stems are covered with pale green leaves which overlap and curl inward.

IDEAL CONDITIONS

Temperature Normal room temperature in summer, even very warm weather suits this plant, but ventilation must be good. Give it a winter rest at 45-50°F/7-10°C.
Light Bright, with direct sun all year.
Water Twice a week in summer but allow the surface of the compost to dry out between waterings. Once a month in winter if the plant is kept in a cool room.
Feed Monthly, spring to early autumn.
Pot-on In spring in loam-based compost.
Propagation Take stem cuttings in summer. Dry them for a day or two before potting.

PROBLEM

Are the leaves turning pale, and are the 'tails' developing straggly, bare growth?

IF YES

CAUSE Not enough light. Sedums require excellent light all year round.
ACTION Move the plant to a windowsill where it will have bright light with direct sun. Plants in hanging containers should also be close to a window.

IF NO

Has the plant been in a warm room in winter?

IF YES

CAUSE The temperature is too high. Plants will continue to grow if they are in warm rooms, but since in winter light is poor, growth is weak and straggly.
ACTION Move the plant to a room in which the temperature is 45-50°F/7-10°C and place it close to a window. At this temperature, growth will virtually stop and the plant will remain in good condition.

PROBLEM

Are the fleshy leaves falling?

IF YES

CAUSE The plant is being handled too frequently; the leaves fall extremely easily.
ACTION Handle the plant as little as possible.

IF NO

Do the leaves also feel soft?

IF YES

CAUSE Overwatering. If the compost is always wet and the leaves are holding all the water they can, they will become soft and bloated.
ACTION Allow the compost almost to dry out, then follow watering instructions in **IDEAL CONDITIONS**.

PROBLEM

Are the leaves shrivelling?

IF YES

CAUSE This is due to underwatering.
ACTION Water the compost thoroughly. In time, the leaves will swell again.

PROBLEM

Are the leaf tips turning brown, and whole leaves curling and falling?

━━━━━━ IF YES ━━━━━━

CAUSE Lack of humidity. Moist air is essential if this plant is to remain looking good during the period of active growth.
ACTION Provide a humid atmosphere: see page 8. Do not mist spray leaves or they will be marked.

━━━━━━ IF NO ━━━━━━

Are the leaves and flowers marked with brown?

━━━━━━ IF YES ━━━━━━

CAUSE Drops of water falling on flowers and foliage, usually when the plant is being watered.
ACTION Instead of watering from above, water by immersion. Place the pot in about 2in/5cm of water and leave for 30 minutes or so. Remove the pot and let excess water drain away.

━━━━━━ IF NO ━━━━━━

Are there green or black insects on stems and the undersides of leaves?

━━━━━━ IF YES ━━━━━━

CAUSE Green or black fly, which suck the sap, making yellow marks that later turn brown.
ACTION Spray the plant with pyrethrum, spraying again every few days if the pests persist. These insects excrete honey dew which encourages sooty mould, a black fungus, to form on the leaves. Wipe it off and tackle the aphids that brought the disease.

━━━━━━ PROBLEM ━━━━━━

After flowering are the leaves beginning to die down?

━━━━━━ IF YES ━━━━━━

CAUSE The natural habit of the plant.
ACTION Gradually reduce the frequency of watering until all the foliage has died down. Cut off the dead leaves and store the tuber completely dry at a temperature of 55°F/13°C. In late winter, break away the old compost and repot in fresh. The tip of the tuber should be level with the compost surface. Water and bring into a temperature of 65-70°F/18-21°C. As new growth appears, increase the frequency of watering.

Sinningia speciosa hybrids
Gloxinias are found in tropical rainforests in Brazil, where temperatures are 75-80°F/24-27°C and rain falls all year. A rosette of velvety mid-green leaves on short, hairy stems surrounds red, pink, white, violet and bi-coloured trumpet-shaped flowers, spring to autumn. After flowering, gloxinias have a dormant period.

IDEAL CONDITIONS

Temperature In summer 60-70°F/16-21°C in a humid atmosphere. In winter, store the tubers at 55°F/13°C.
Light Bright, but not direct sunlight. Stored tubers need no light.
Water Two or three times a week in summer. As the leaves die down after the plant has flowered, water less often; when they are dead, stop watering.
Feed Every two weeks from late spring until leaves begin to die.
Pot-on Every three or four years in late winter. Repot in fresh compost every year.
Propagation Stem cuttings in summer.

Solanum capicastrum
The winter cherry is from grassland areas of Brazil. Temperatures in summer are 75°F/24°C; in winter down to 50-55°F/10-13°C. Most rain falls in summer, winter is fairly dry. Many small stems of dark green oval leaves branch off the main stem. Small white flowers in summer, become green berries that turn yellow, then bright red.

IDEAL CONDITIONS

Temperature Normal room temperatures in summer. If possible put plants outdoors. In winter, rest them around 50°F/10°C, but up to 60°F/16°C will be tolerated.
Light Bright, but out of direct sun in summer. Weak winter sun does no harm.
Water Two or three times a week in summer so compost is always moist. Every 10 to 14 days in winter to prevent drying out.
Feed Every two weeks, from late spring to early autumn.
Pot-on In spring in loam-based compost.
Propagation Sow seed in spring.

PROBLEM

Are the leaves limp and falling, and is fruit beginning to drop shortly after turning red? Is the plant in a warm centrally heated room?

IF YES

CAUSE The temperature is too high. If the plant is kept cool, the berries should last for many weeks.
ACTION Move the plant to a room in which the temperature is 50-60°F/10-16°C.

IF NO

Is the plant in a shaded part of the room?

IF YES

CAUSE Not enough light. Berries will last much longer if they have some direct sunlight in winter.
ACTION Move the plant to a windowsill with direct sun.

IF NO

When you push a finger into the compost does it feel dry about 2in/5cm down?

IF YES

CAUSE Underwatering. Although this plant needs less frequent watering in winter the compost should never be allowed to dry out completely.
ACTION Water the compost thoroughly. In future, follow watering instructions in **IDEAL CONDITIONS**.

IF NO

Is the atmosphere in the room dry?

IF YES

CAUSE Lack of humidity. This is more likely to be a problem if the plant is kept at the upper end of the temperature range in winter.
ACTION Create a humid atmosphere: see page 8. Mist spray the leaves.

IF NO

Have the leaves started to fall in late winter?

IF YES

CAUSE Natural growth cycle of the plant.
ACTION After the berries have fallen, cut back all stems by two-thirds. Pinch out growing tips to encourage bushy growth. In late spring put the plant outdoors in a shady spot.

◁ PROBLEM ▷

Are the leaf tips turning brown, and do the leaves have brown patches? Is the plant always in a warm room?

IF YES

CAUSE A combination of warmth and dry air.
ACTION Provide humidity for plants if the temperature is much above 60°F/16°C: see page 8.

IF NO

Has the plant been exposed to direct sunlight?

IF YES

CAUSE The leaves have been scorched. Sparmannias require good light but should be shaded from the sun.
ACTION Move the plant to a position where it has bright light but is out of the direct line of the sun.

IF NO

Are the leaves also limp and wilting? Does the compost feel dry just below the surface?

IF YES

CAUSE Underwatering.
ACTION Thoroughly water the compost. If the compost has shrunk from the sides of the pot, immerse it in a pail of water to within 2in/5cm of the rim. Leave for about 30 minutes.

PROBLEM

Are the leaves turning pale, and is growth lanky?

IF YES

CAUSE Not enough light, especially in the short daylight hours of winter.
ACTION Move the plant closer to a window where it will have good light, but no direct sun.

PROBLEM

Is the plant growing quickly and becoming too large for the room?

IF YES

CAUSE This is the natural growth of the plant, but overlarge plants can be kept in check.
ACTION After flowering, cut down all stems by half. When new growth is underway, pinch out growing tips to encourage bushy growth.

Sparmannia africana
Sparmannia is a shrub from subtropical forest areas of South Africa. Summer temperatures are 65-70°F/18-21°C, down to 55°F/13°C in winter. Rain falls all year, but is heaviest in autumn and winter. In the northern hemisphere the plant needs watering often in summer. Bright green hairy leaves; white flowers with purple stamens in late spring.

IDEAL CONDITIONS

Temperature In summer, 60-65°F/16-18°C. Rest the plant in winter at 50-55°F/10-13°C.
Light Bright, but never in direct sun.
Water Two or three times a week in summer so the compost is evenly moist. Once a week in winter; but if the plant is kept warmer than recommended, water more often.
Feed Every two weeks, late spring to early autumn.
Pot-on Each year after flowering in a loam-based compost. Young plants grow fast and may need potting-on twice a year.
Propagation Stem cuttings in late spring.

Spathiphyllum wallisii
Spathiphyllums are native to the rain forests of Colombia which have temperatures of 75-80°F/24-27°C all year, as well as rain and high humidity. Glossy, bright green leaves are carried on short stalks. Flowers, produced in spring to late summer, are similar to lilies: an oval white spathe surrounding a yellow spadix.

IDEAL CONDITIONS

Temperature In summer, 65-70°F/18-21°C. The plant does better if rested in winter at 60-65°F/16-18°C. It needs humidity.
Light Bright, but no direct sun.
Water Two or three times a week in summer to ensure compost is always moist. Once a week in winter if the temperature is lower.
Feed Every two weeks, late spring to early autumn.
Pot-on In spring, in loam- or peat-based compost.
Propagation Divide the rhizome when potting-on. Each piece should have several leaves and a good root system.

PROBLEM

Do the leaves have brown edges or brown papery markings over their surface? Is the plant in a warm, dry centrally heated room?

IF YES

CAUSE Insufficient humidity.
ACTION Create a humid atmosphere: see page 8. Regular mist-spraying of the leaves helps.

IF NO

Has the plant been exposed to direct sunlight?

IF YES

CAUSE The leaves have been scorched.
ACTION Move the plant out of direct sunlight to a place where it still gets bright light. Remove any badly marked leaves at compost level.

IF NO

Are there fine white webs on the stems and leaves?

IF YES

CAUSE Red spider mites, usually encouraged by dry air. They suck the sap, leaving yellow marks which later turn brown.
ACTION Wipe away webs and spray the plant with liquid derris, concentrating on the undersides of the leaves. Repeat every few days if the pests persist. Keep them at bay by increasing humidity.

PROBLEM

Has the plant failed to flower?

IF YES

CAUSE Not enough light. In the build-up to the flowering period this plant requires as bright a light as possible during the short daylight hours of winter.
ACTION Move the plant close to a window but keep it out of direct sun.

IF NO

Has the plant been in an unheated room in winter?

IF YES

CAUSE It has been too cold.
ACTION Nothing immediately, but next winter make sure that if the plant is rested the temperature does not fall below 60°F/16°C.

PROBLEM

Has the plant produced fewer buds than in previous years, and have the buds fallen?

IF YES

CAUSE Not enough light. If plants are to flower well they need bright light all year round.
ACTION Move the plant closer to a window, where the light is good but there is no fierce direct sun.

IF NO

Has the plant been moved about when in bud?

IF YES

CAUSE Just that; when in bud it should not be disturbed.
ACTION None for the moment, but next year leave the plant exactly where it is when buds begin to develop.

IF NO

After flowering have complete spurs been cut off?

IF YES

CAUSE This greatly reduces the number of flowers in the future, since new growth appears from the spurs.
ACTION Allow flowers and stalks to fall naturally.

IF NO

Does the compost feel dry about 2in/5cm down?

IF YES

CAUSE The compost had been allowed to dry out.
ACTION Follow watering instructions in **IDEAL CONDITIONS**.

IF NO

Is the atmosphere in the room dry?

IF YES

CAUSE Lack of humidity.
ACTION Increase humidity: see page 8.

IF NO

Are there soft, light brown or hard, dark brown bumps on the undersides of the leaves?

IF YES

CAUSE An infestation of scale insects.
ACTION Scrape them off with a fingernail. For heavy infestations repeat spray with malathion.

Stephanotis floribunda
Stephanotis is a climbing shrub from tropical rain forests of Madagascar. Rain falls all year, the air is always moist and temperatures are 70-80°F/21-27°C. Opposite pairs of tough, shiny evergreen leaves grow on long stems, and there are clusters of fragrant, white, waxy flowers in late spring and early summer.

IDEAL CONDITIONS

Temperature In summer around 70°F/21°C. Rest the plant in winter at 55°F/13°C. Needs extra humidity in warm weather.
Light Bright, but not direct sunlight.
Water Two or three times a week in summer. About once a week in winter if in a cool room, more often if kept warm.
Feed Every two weeks, late spring to early autumn.
Pot-on In spring in a peat- or loam-based compost.
Propagation Take stem cuttings in spring, but avoid those with flower buds. In order to root they need bottom heat of 70°F/21°C.

Streptocarpus hybrids
The Cape primrose is from temperate forest areas of Cape Province, S. Africa, with summers 65-70°F/18-21°C, winters a little cooler. There is no dry season, but most rain falls in winter. Dark green strap-shaped leaves form a rosette. There are clusters of five-lobed red, pink, white or purple flowers, spring to autumn.

IDEAL CONDITIONS

Temperature In summer, 65-70°F/ 18-21°C. Rest it in winter down to 55°F/13°C. It needs humidity, especially in hot weather.
Light Bright, but never direct sunlight.
Water Two or three times a week in summer, but let the surface of the compost dry out between waterings. In winter every 7 to 10 days; less often at low temperatures.
Feed Every two weeks, late spring to early autumn.
Pot-on After the plant has flowered; use a peat-based compost.
Propagation Take leaf cuttings in summer. Or sow seed in spring.

PROBLEM

Are the leaf edges turning brown and are leaves shrivelling, curling and falling? Are temperatures consistently high?

IF YES

CAUSE The air is too dry. The higher the temperature, the more essential humidity becomes.
ACTION Create a humid atmosphere: see page 8.

IF NO

Does the compost feel dry about 2in/5cm down?

IF YES

CAUSE The compost has been allowed to dry out.
ACTION Thoroughly water the compost. Thereafter, follow watering instructions in **IDEAL CONDITIONS**.

IF NO

Are the leaf stems brown and mushy at the point where they emerge from the compost?

IF YES

CAUSE Stem rot, often encouraged by a combination of low temperature and sodden compost during the winter rest period.
ACTION Remove the rotting stems and dust the compost with fungicide powder. Allow the compost to dry out and then follow watering instructions in **IDEAL CONDITIONS**. Move the plant to a warmer room.

IF NO

Is there also a white powder on the leaves?

IF YES

CAUSE This is mildew, which often strikes when humidity is high but ventilation poor.
ACTION Remove any badly infected leaves and spray with benomyl. Repeat every few days if the disease persists. Increase ventilation.

IF NO

Are there green insects on flower stalks and buds?

IF YES

CAUSE Greenfly, which suck the sap from the plant and cause distorted growth.
ACTION Spray the plant with pyrethrum and respray every few days if necessary.

PROBLEM

Are the leaves turning brown and papery and shrivelling? Is the plant in a warm room throughout the year?

───────── IF YES ─────────

CAUSE Lack of humidity. If temperatures are always high, humidity is essential.
ACTION Create a humid atmosphere: see page 8.

───────── IF NO ─────────

Does the compost feel dry about 2in/5cm down?

───────── IF YES ─────────

CAUSE Underwatering.
ACTION Thoroughly water the compost. In future water as in **IDEAL CONDITIONS**. In the wild the aerial roots also draw on water and nutrients to support the plant's growth. To provide extra moisture insert the aerial roots in a moss stick which is kept constantly moist.

───────── IF NO ─────────

Are the browning leaves touching a wall?

───────── IF YES ─────────

CAUSE Plaster, which is a very absorbent material, is drawing moisture from the leaves.
ACTION Move the plant away from the wall.

PROBLEM

Are the leaves losing their contrasting colouring?

───────── IF YES ─────────

CAUSE Not enough light.
ACTION Move the plant closer to a window where it will have bright light but no direct sun.

───────── IF NO ─────────

Are the leaves looking generally pale, almost yellow?

───────── IF YES ─────────

CAUSE Either the plant requires potting-on or has not been fed regularly. As the roots fill the pot they displace the compost, which provides food for the plant.
ACTION Remove the plant from the pot and if it is filled with roots pot-on to the next size. Feed regularly after about three months, when the compost's nutrients have been exhausted.

Syngonium podophyllum
The climber syngonium is from the tropical rain forests of Central America, with temperatures all year 70-75°F/21-24°C, regular rain and air always moist. The leaves, shaped like arrowheads, have three lobes on a young plant, up to seven when it is mature. They are dark green, with lighter colouring around the veins.

IDEAL CONDITIONS

Temperature In summer 65-70°F/18-21°C. In winter the plant will tolerate down to 60°F/16°C.
Light Bright, but no direct sun at any time. Sunlight filtered through a blind or curtain will do no harm.
Water Two or three times a week in summer, but let the surface of the compost dry out before rewatering.
Feed Every two weeks from late spring to early autumn.
Pot-on In spring in mixture of loam compost and leaf mould or peat.
Propagation Take stem cuttings in late spring.

T
O
L
M
I
E
A

Tolmiea menziesii
Tolmieas come from wooded areas of the American west coast, California in particular. Summer is usually 60-70°F/16-21°C but can be much warmer, winter (when most rain falls) mild, 50°F/10°C. Hairy, bright green leaves grow on short stalks and small plantlets form at the junction of leaf and stalk.

IDEAL CONDITIONS

Temperature In summer, 55-60°F/ 13-16°C. Rest the plant in winter at 50°F/10°C.
Light Bright, but not direct sunlight. Tolmieas will tolerate a slightly shady spot.
Water Two to three times a week in summer so the compost is always moist. Every 7 or 10 days in winter.
Feed Every two weeks from late spring to early autumn.
Pot-on In spring in peat-based compost.
Propagation By pinning down into compost a leaf with a plantlet attached in late spring/early summer.

PROBLEM

Are the leaves limp and shrivelling? If you push a finger into the compost does it feel dry below the surface?

IF YES

CAUSE Not enough water.
ACTION Water the compost thoroughly. In warm weather a tolmiea may need frequent watering. In future, water as in **IDEAL CONDITIONS**.

IF NO

Is the atmosphere in the room dry and warm?

IF YES

CAUSE Lack of humidity, especially during very warm weather.
ACTION Create humidity around the plant: see page 8. Frequent mist spraying of the leaves also helps.

IF NO

Are there fine white webs on the leaves and stems, and are the leaves covered with a white powder?

IF YES

CAUSE Red spider mites, which suck the sap, leaving yellow marks on the leaves. They are encouraged by the dry atmosphere in poorly ventilated warm rooms.
ACTION Wipe off the webs and powder with a damp cloth. Spray the plant with liquid derris and repeat every few days if the mites persist. To keep the pests at bay, increase humidity and improve ventilation.

PROBLEM

Is growth generally weak, with long leaf stalks, and is the foliage turning pale?

IF YES

CAUSE Insufficient light. Tolmieas will grow in slight shade, but this will be the result if it is too dark.
ACTION Move the plant closer to a window, where the light is good, but out of the direct line of the sun. If the plant is getting old, it may be better to start off new plants and discard the old one. Either remove a leaf with a plantlet, shorten the stalk to 2in/5cm and insert it into compost, or pin down in compost a leaf still attached to the main plant, where it joins the stalk. Sever from the main plant when established. Plant several rooted plantlets in a pot for a bushy show.

PROBLEM

Are leaf tips or whole leaves turning brown, shrivelling and dropping? Does the compost feel dry about 2in/5cm down?

Tradescantia fulminensis 'Quicksilver'

Tradescantias are from tropical rainforests of S. America, particularly Brazil, where they creep along the forest floor. Rain falls all year, air is moist and temperatures 75-80°F/24-27°C. A good plant for hanging baskets, its long trailing stems bear oval green leaves with narrow white stripes in spring and summer.

IF YES

CAUSE The plant is not getting enough water.
ACTION Thoroughly water the compost. If the compost has shrunk from the side of the pot, it is better to immerse the pot in a pail of water to within 2in/5cm of the pot rim. Leave for 30 minutes, then remove the pot and leave it to drain. In future follow watering instructions in **IDEAL CONDITIONS**.

IF NO

Is the plant always in a warm room in winter?

IF YES

CAUSE The air is too dry.
ACTION If plants are grown in a hanging container, mist spray the leaves daily. If in a pot, stand the pot on a tray of wet pebbles or surround it with moist peat.

PROBLEM

Is growth becoming weak, with bare lower stems, and are leaves losing their contrasting colouring?

IF YES

CAUSE Insufficient light, especially during the short daylight hours of winter.
ACTION Move the plant closer to a window, where it will have bright light with some direct sun but not hot midday sun. Any stems which carry plain green leaves should be cut away at compost level, otherwise the whole plant may revert to plain green. Cut back any bare stems to compost level and regularly pinch out growing tips to encourage bushy growth.

IF NO

Have you had the plant for two or more years?

IF YES

CAUSE Tradescantia plants of this age are old.
ACTION Now is the time to create a new, healthy plant by propagation. Take stem cuttings about 4in/10cm long and plant several in compost in the same pot to make a bushy display. Cuttings may also be rooted in water and then, when roots have developed, planted in compost.

IDEAL CONDITIONS

Temperature In summer, 65-70°F/ 18-21°C. Rest the plant in winter as low as 50°F/10°C.
Light Bright, some direct sun all year unless scorching.
Water Two or three times a week in summer to keep compost evenly moist. Once a week in winter; more often in a warm room.
Feed Every two weeks, late spring to early autumn.
Pot-on After two or three years in spring in loam- or peat-based compost. Replace old plants by cuttings instead of potting-on again.
Propagation Take stem cuttings in spring or summer.

Vriesea splendens
Vrieseas are epiphytic bromeliads which grow on tree branches and rocks in tropical forests of Brazil. The climate is humid and warm, 75-80°F/24-27°C. In the wild, food and water collect in the central rosette of dark green, strap-shaped leaves. A spike of overlapping red bracts with yellow flowers appears in summer.

IDEAL CONDITIONS

Temperature All year at 65-75°F/18-24°C; even in winter not below 65°F/18°C. Needs a humid atmosphere.
Light Bright, with some direct sun. Shade from fierce midday sun.
Water Two or three times a week in summer so compost is evenly moist; keep the central rosette filled with water. Once a week in winter and keep the central rosette dry.
Feed Monthly, spring to early autumn.
Pot-on Every two or three years in a mixture of sphagnum moss, peat and sand.
Propagation Remove well-developed off-sets when potting-on.

PROBLEM

Are the leaf tips turning brown and papery? Is the atmosphere in the room always dry?

IF YES

CAUSE Insufficient humidity.
ACTION Create a humid atmosphere: see page 8. Daily mist spraying also helps.

IF NO

Has the compost been allowed to dry out, and has the central rosette been kept dry during summer?

IF YES

CAUSE Underwatering. In summer, compost should be moist always, but not waterlogged.
ACTION Thoroughly water the compost. Keep the central rosette topped up with water. In future water as in **IDEAL CONDITIONS**.

IF NO

Are there also brown markings on the leaves?

IF YES

CAUSE The leaves have been scorched; they should not be exposed to very fierce sun.
ACTION Move the plant so that it is out of the direct line of midday sun or provide some form of shading.

PROBLEM

Is the colour of the bracts fading quickly, and have flowers failed to appear? Is the plant in the shade?

IF YES

CAUSE Not enough light.
ACTION Move the plant closer to a brightly lit window.

PROBLEM

Is the rosette dying back after it has produced bracts and flowers?

IF YES

CAUSE This is the natural life cycle for this plant. Before it dies completely, it will throw out small offsets from the base of the plant.
ACTION When the offsets are well established and at least 6in/15cm tall, with a good root system, cut them away from the parent plant.

PROBLEM

Are the outer leaves of the rosette turning yellow, shrivelling and then falling? Is the plant in a shaded part of the room?

IF YES

CAUSE The plant is not getting enough light.
ACTION Remove any badly discoloured leaves. Move the plant close to a sunny window. If possible, put it outdoors in summer in a sheltered, sunny spot. Remember to bring it indoors before the first autumn frosts. In the short hours of winter daylight it needs all the sun it can get.

IF NO

Are the leaf tips turning brown before the whole leaf yellows? Are the tips of the leaves touching a wall?

IF YES

CAUSE Wall plaster, which is very absorbent, is drawing moisture from the leaves of the plant.
ACTION Move the plant away from the wall. Remove any badly marked leaves cleanly from the rosette.

IF NO

Are there soft, light brown or hard, dark brown bumps on the undersides of the leaves?

IF YES

CAUSE These are scale insects, which suck the sap from the leaves.
ACTION If there are only a few, scrape them off with a fingernail. Spray badly infested plants with malathion, repeating every few days if the pests persist.

PROBLEM

Is the plant the same height as when you bought it?

IF YES

CAUSE Entirely natural. The trunk will never grow any taller, but it should produce new rosettes of leaves. The stems of this plant are cut into lengths by nurserymen and induced to root. The taller plants are, the more expensive they come.

OTHER SPECIES

Yucca aloifolia has similar rosettes of leaves, but they are edged with fine teeth.

Yucca elephantipes
Yuccas are found in arid areas of Mexico, where summers are hot and winters about 45°F/7°C. Rainfall is low and unpredictable, so yuccas put down long roots to obtain water. Sections of this plant stem are cut into pieces and induced to root to make yucca cane plants. The stout trunk bears rosettes of sword-shaped leaves.

IDEAL CONDITIONS

Temperature In summer 55-65°F/13-18°C, but a yucca will tolerate any amount of heat. Rest the plant in winter, about 50°F/10°C and not below 45°F/7°C.
Light Bright with direct sun all year.
Water Two or three times a week in summer. Every 7 to 10 days in winter.
Feed Every two weeks from late spring to early autumn.
Pot-on In spring every other year in two parts loam-based compost to one part sand.
Propagation By taking a rosette of leaves, but this spoils the shape of the plant.

Zebrina pendula
'Quadricolor'
Zebrinas creep along the ground and up the trunks of trees in their forest home in Mexico. It is warm all year, 70-75°F/21-24°C, and the air is always moist. The oval green leaves, striped cream, pink and silver and with undersides of purple, show best in a hanging container.

IDEAL CONDITIONS

Temperature
65-70°F/18-21°C all year but a winter rest will do no harm if not below 55°F/13°C.
Light Bright with direct sun all year, except when fierce.
Water Twice a week in summer; let the surface dry out before watering again. Once a week in winter so compost is barely moist; less often if resting.
Feed Every two weeks, from late spring to early autumn.
Pot-on In spring in peat-based compost; but best to replace the plant after two years.
Propagation Take stem cuttings in spring and summer.

PROBLEM

Are leaf tips or whole leaves turning brown? When you push a finger into the compost does it feel dry about 2in/5cm down?

IF YES

CAUSE Underwatering.
ACTION Thoroughly water the compost. In future, water as in **IDEAL CONDITIONS**.

IF NO

Is the plant close to a window which gets several hours of direct sun?

IF YES

CAUSE The plant has been exposed to midday sun.
ACTION Move the plant to a position in which it will have sun at the beginning or end of the day.

IF NO

Is the atmosphere in the room dry, especially in winter?

IF YES

CAUSE Lack of humidity.
ACTIONS Stand the pot on a tray of wet pebbles or surround it with moist peat. Plants in hanging containers should be mist sprayed daily.

PROBLEM

Has growth become weak and straggly and is leaf colour fading? Is the plant in the shade?

IF YES

CAUSE Not enough light.
ACTION Move the plant closer to a window where it will have bright light with some direct sun. Cut back any bare stems to compost level and regularly pinch out growing tips to encourage bushy growth. Any stems with plain green leaves should be removed.

IF NO

Have you had the plant for two or more years?

IF YES

CAUSE The plant is getting old.
ACTION Raise new plants by taking cuttings, which will root in compost or water. Several cuttings should be planted in the same pot to give a bushy effect.

CREDITS

Andrew Bicknell and George Seddon are
authors both jointly and individually of six
other books on houseplants and gardening.

Plant illustrations on pages 18-32
by Will Giles.

Illustrations on pages 6-17
by Nicki Kemball.

Typesetting and origination by
Modern Reprographics Ltd,
Harpings Road, Hull, North Humberside.